Advance Praise

"The new rules for branding in the 21st century come down to one word: authenticity. Re Perez's book provides a beautiful blend of the art and science of branding, whether you're a global enterprise or an emerging entrepreneur who's disrupting the status quo."

—YANIK SILVER, AUTHOR, *EVOLVED ENTERPRISE* AND FOUNDER, MAVERICK1000

"From my experience working with eight-figure companies—the ones that grow every year—it has everything to do with their brand. Re Perez has helped many of my friends build power-house brands. I strongly recommend you figuratively, 'come out of the closet' and devour this book right away."

—MICHAEL LOVITCH, CO-FOUNDER, THE BABY BATHWATER INSTITUTE

"This book, like its author, is unique and full of amazing insights. Re Perez provides small business owners and marketing teams with actionable branding insights and a proven methodology to transform your brand and dominate the market."

—DANIEL MARCOS, CEO, GROWTH INSTITUTE

"When it comes to branding and authenticity, there's no one I know who exudes more brilliance in both than Re Perez. He has a unique ability to blend his strategic and creative thinking with his heart and soul."

—RYAN DEISS, CO-FOUNDER OF DIGITAL MARKETER

"There is the mind of your business and then there's the heart and soul. Re Perez is one of the smartest minds in branding, helping entrepreneurs get connected to the heart and soul. This book is his gift to all of us!"

—NICHOLAS KUSMICH, WORLD'S TOP
FACEBOOK ADS STRATEGIST

"If you want to uncover the coolest, most innovative, and utmost authentic version of your brand, this book will show you the way. You won't want to put it down because you'll fall in love with who you'll discover your brand to be."

—SUZANNE EVANS, *NEW YORK TIMES*
BESTSELLER, *INC.* 500 HONOR ROLL

"This book, like its author, challenges you to think in a different mindset than you are used to and comfortable with...it's a big stretch, however it's one that you will not regret. Embrace this book and implement the ideas contained within...you will never look back!!!"

—HOWARD O'MEARA, CHAIRMAN OF
CHANGING HABITS (AUSTRALIA)

"*Re Perez cuts through all the jargon and hype to deliver a compelling and authentic brand experience that delivers increased revenue, regardless of the size of your business. Whether you read this book or see Re in person, your life will be changed for the better.*"

—NATHAN BAILEY, MANAGING DIRECTOR
OF CHANGING HABITS (AUSTRALIA)

"*We hired two other branding companies before meeting Re Perez. His approach was easier to understand. He had a better process and worked with the entire team to come up with a brand that got everyone excited. He will satisfy you and your team completely.*"

—CRAIG HANDLEY, CEO OF LISTENTRUST AND
BEST-SELLING AUTHOR OF *HIRED TO QUIT*

"*Working with Re Perez on my branding was arguably one of the most important things I did for my business. He set us on a path forward, clarified things for my team, and unified our message at every point—from who we talk to, how we talk to them, and what we stand for.*"

—RAJ JANA, CEO AND FOUNDER OF
JAVAPRESSE AND STAY GROUNDED

"*Re Perez is one of the smartest big-thinkers I know in the branding space. In working with him and following his process, my brand grew up and futurized. He put real meaning, direction,* and structure around my brand. I even up-leveled as a human being."

—SHANDA SUMPTER, CEO AND FOUNDER OF HEARTCORE BUSINESS

"This book does for your business what full self-expression does for the soul. Re Perez shares the secrets behind discovering the soul of your business through discovering the soul of your authentic self. This book will show you step-by-step how to dig deep, innovate, and create an authentic brand people love."

—MALORIE TADIMI, ENTREPRENEUR AND FOUNDER OF MALORIE.COM

"I connect with the most successful individuals in digital marketing every single month. So when great talent comes around, it's easy to spot. Re Perez has that level of talent. This book will challenge how you think about branding. Read it before your competitors do."

—DAVID GONZALEZ, FOUNDER OF INTERNET MARKETING PARTY

"Re Perez is masterful at his craft. His process is genius. His innate abilities are rare and can't be taught. If the term unicorn is used to describe a true master whose talent is one in a million, Re is a unicorn's unicorn. He is truly one of the most remarkable beings walking on the planet."

—DAN HYMAN, LIGHTWORKER AND FOUNDER OF INFINITE BEGINNINGS

"*Working with Re Perez has been one of the best business investments I have ever made. I went from blending in with everyone else to instantly being positioned as the sought-after thought leader within my industry. If you want to crush the competition, then hire Re.*"

—NICK UNSWORTH, CEO AND FOUNDER OF LIFE ON FIRE

"*Re Perez is a true professional with an extraordinary vision to differentiate your company and take your business to an entirely new level. If you're looking to set yourself apart from the pack, then I recommend Re.*"

—MARIA ANDROS-BUCKLEY, BUSINESS
AND MARKETING STRATEGIST

"*Re Perez is the real deal when it comes to authentic branding. After branding our company with Re, we were able to grow our events by 300%, charge four times more for our programs, and make it easier to scale our business.*"

—BRENT WEAVER, CEO AND FOUNDER OF UGURUS

"*Working with Re Perez enabled us to reposition our company into exactly where we wanted to go by adding several layers to our business.*"

—AFRIN KHAN, CEO AND FOUNDER OF RED ELEPHANT, INC.

"*Rebranding can be a pain in the ass process for a company. Our new brand opened up more markets for us to sell into and really gave us a bigger company image to fulfill our vision for growth. Re Perez wowed my team with his proven branding process.*"

—TONY RICCIARDI, CO-FOUNDER OF LISTENTRUST

"In a noisy world, there are all kinds of manipulative techniques used to get more likes and followers. Re Perez's book is a gift for people to see themselves more clearly and embrace their uniqueness, rather than trying to change to match the masses."

—CHRISTINE KANE, CEO AND FOUNDER OF UPLEVEL YOU

"Working with Re Perez has made a huge impact on us personally and professionally. I have never experienced such an in-depth branding process. There is no comparison in the industry."

—DEBRA BERNDT-MALDONADO, CO-FOUNDER OF THE CENTER OF JUNGIAN POSITIVE PSYCHOLOGY

"Re Perez helped me create a company that couldn't be more me. Sales has become so easy because my brand is beautiful and compelling, and my ideal clients really know when I'm talking to them now."

—JULIE SEROT, THE DHARMA CIRCLE

Your Brand Should Be Gay
(Even If You're Not)

Your Brand Should Be Gay

(even if you're not)

The Art and Science of
Creating an Authentic Brand

Re Perez

LIONCREST

YOUR BRAND SHOULD BE GAY (EVEN IF YOU'RE NOT)

The Art and Science of Creating an Authentic Brand

ISBN   978-1-5445-0333-2 *Hardcover*

978-1-5445-0331-8 *Paperback*

978-1-5445-0332-5 *Ebook*

Contents

Introduction

THE GREY CEILING

"You know, Re, you just don't have enough gray hair."

I was in my early thirties sitting across from the global Human Resources Director at one of the top global branding firms where I had worked for over three years. I had just asked about a promotion.

I couldn't believe the words that were coming out of her mouth. She continued on to say that even though I was clearly committed, driven, and good at my job, I didn't look old enough. I needed to look a certain age and have a particular stature in order to be seen as credible in the eyes of the C-Suite and Fortune 500 executive clients. Ironically, several of my colleagues were chronologically younger than me, but because they looked older, they had already joined the ranks above me.

I was devastated.

But, in that moment, I learned that perception is everything! No matter how solid one's qualifications or credentials, people's perception matters more.

For context, I was thrilled to be working in the branding industry. And, in particular, this consulting firm, which housed some of the smartest and brightest Brand Strategists and creative professionals in the world. Admittedly though, I also found the work culture toxic and ego-centric. It was about getting ahead, even at the cost of someone else's career. My colleagues focused on winning the "politics" game, not being the most creative or smartest. It was about thriving in a "sink or swim" world (and there were quite a few sharks in the water), rather than in a collaborative, supportive culture.

I was at a crossroads in my career. I wouldn't be able to advance (at least at this company), but I didn't want to abandon the foundation I'd created. I loved every minute of branding. And, I felt I was naturally good at it.

But, as things go, several months later, I got pulled into a meeting. You know, the kind of meeting where they sit you down, close the doors, and tell you (in an emotionless manner) that you're being laid off from your position due to "corporate restructuring."

Essentially, I was fired.

It was the final piece of evidence that confirmed I was doomed to sink at this company, no matter how well I swam. I knew deep in my soul I had a lot more to contribute to a company like this, but I didn't want to play the victim. I decided to move on. In the years following my departure, I landed positions at smaller branding agencies and consulting firms—in roles that would seem like "promotions" or "career advancement." I was offered more money and even assigned high-ranking titles. The only problem: I wasn't fully challenged at these companies or in these positions. Something was still missing.

FROM HEARTBREAK TO BREAKTHROUGH

I was starting to discover that more money and a fancy title were not truly fulfilling. I began a quest to find other ways to feel fulfilled. I considered leaving New York City to live in another country. Maybe that would be my next move? I even thought that finding love and being in a romantic relationship would fill the void I was experiencing.

As it were, both opportunities showed up—simultaneously!

A friend recommended I explore online dating but instead of limiting prospects to New York City, leave the geographic filters to include the rest of the world. After a couple of interactions, I connected with one man over the phone because he lived in South Dakota. In one conversation, we instantaneously fell in love. This attraction was beyond what I had ever experienced before. So, I started to organize my life around starting a life with this man.

Shortly thereafter, one of the top international branding firms asked if I would consider working in Dubai, U.A.E.

My first thought was: "relationship *or* career?" But, I kept considering the question until I had coached myself to think "relationship *and* career."

After long-distance dating for only five months, we decided to take the risk and move to Dubai together. We packed up our things, said our goodbyes to our families, and settled into our apartment in Dubai Media City. As luck would have it, the romantic story didn't go as planned. After only one week in Dubai, my partner became cold and distant. He found out that his father was diagnosed with stage four liver cancer. The romantic journey we were on suddenly ended. We broke up that week.

Understandably, he needed to go back to the States and be with his dad. I knew it was the right thing for him to do, but still, I was despondent. For some reason, this break up shook me to my core. It took me on a downward spiral of depression and self-doubt. Here I was living in a new country with no family or support structure—just my new work colleagues. I felt suffocated, lost, and heartbroken. I started to question everything: What am I doing out here? What am I really doing with my life? Why do I continue to find myself in a position of unfulfillment and sorrow both in my personal life and professional career?

It was time to make a change. It was time for a transformation. I decided to leave my new job, return to New York City, and take time to heal my broken heart and figure out life. In the subsequent six months, I went on an inward journey to find a deeper purpose in my life, which involved many hours of reading, journaling, yoga, and meditation every day. I even went on a retreat in Sedona, Arizona, which is where I got in touch with spirituality.

Finally, in early December 2010, I had a breakthrough. I got clear on what was next for me: I would create my own branding firm. And, I wanted to help smaller companies that were making a difference and positively impacting people's lives.

This led me to entrepreneurship. In January 2011, I launched Branding For The People.

FROM EMPLOYEE TO ENTREPRENEUR

I didn't exactly know how to run a business, but I was determined not to be another cog-in-the-wheel employee again. In creating a separation from the Fortune 500 environment, I quickly found myself surrounded by entrepreneurs and small business owners. I started to observe their way of thinking and approach to building businesses—as well as their branding.

I remember thinking that their entire approach to branding couldn't have been more different to that of the Fortune 500 companies I was accustomed to. I couldn't help but negatively critique their lack of a clear message, poorly designed logos, confusing marketing copy, non-functional websites, and even their ink-jet-printed business cards.

I felt compelled to tell them candidly and unabashedly to STOP doing what they're doing because it was just *so bad*. I offered suggestions on how they could make their branding better, clearer, and more professional. While you'd think most people would get easily hurt or offended, I got a different response. My new entrepreneurial friends were appreciative. It was the first time someone was direct and brutally honest with them, while at the same time able to provide valuable tips and constructive ideas on how to improve.

My biggest takeaway: Entrepreneurs and small businesses "don't know what they didn't know" when it comes to branding. They either didn't know "branding" even existed, or they thought branding was synonymous with marketing or logo design. They couldn't grasp that branding is both an art (design, colors, graphics, imagery, fonts) and science (psychology, sociology, cognitive linguistics). Everything about branding that came so natural to me was completely revolutionary to them. They were astounded by the depth of my training and knowledge in the field. Their acknowledgment of my expertise wasn't what amazed me. Rather, it was the look in their eyes and their physiology shift when they began to see the world differently. It was as if I had given them their first pair of prescription glasses, and they could see clear shapes at a great distance. They began to understand the art and science behind the process. Branding became a "want" they hadn't even known they wanted. Inevitably, they would ask if they could hire me to build their brand.

When I received my first check from a client, I quietly celebrated and told myself: "I'm now in business." Because I now had "proof of concept" that small businesses could benefit from my Fortune 500 background and experience.

MY RELATIONSHIP WITH PERCEPTION

I often get asked the question: "Why are you so *passionate* about branding?" Most people assumed it was because branding is considered "cool," "creative," and "fun." While all that's true and certainly makes the profession exciting and enjoyable, the answer lies within my deeper relationship with the power of "perception"—because branding is all about creating perception. Whether we're aware of it or not, people form perceptions about us all the time, and to some degree, we all care about how others perceive us.

Like many kids in their formative years of high school, I cared about my classmates' perceptions of me. I wanted to fit in. I wanted to be accepted. At the same time, I didn't want to fit in at the expense of being true to myself. But the pressure of wanting to fit in during high school was compounded for me by three layers:

I attended an all-boys Catholic Jesuit high school on financial aid.

I was the son of divorced parents, raised by a single mom.

And, deep down, I knew that I was gay.

My mother was always concerned with my brother's and my education. She wanted the best for us. She pushed for us to get into a private Jesuit high school, even though we couldn't afford it. My mom was the sole breadwinner, as my parents divorced when I was fourteen (but later remarried when I was twenty-one). Thankfully, the school had a motto that no child with academic qualifications would be turned down because of finances. Because my brother and

I had the grades and smarts to attend, we were accepted under the condition that we complete several hours of community service a week—something most of our friends, who came from rich families, would never have to experience. Already, we came into a culture in which we didn't seem to fit. At least, economically.

Then, of course, you layer on the fact that we came from what was arguably seen as a "broken" family. All of our friends seemed to have the "perfect" moms and dads. They drove around in their Range Rovers, Corvettes, or Ferraris. They wore the nicest clothes and signature brands of the time (e.g., Polo/Ralph Lauren, Dockers, and Sperry). And, when they weren't studying or playing after-school sports, they frequently hosted swanky dance parties in their homes. We couldn't afford nice clothes. We couldn't have our friends over for parties in our tiny two-bedroom apartment. These were all luxuries that my brother and I couldn't participate in. In addition to our obligatory community service, we worked part time (to help our mom pay the bills). Consequently, it was time-prohibitive for us to participate in sports or other extracurricular activities. Finally, for me, in particular, I knew that I was different. I was attracted to my classmates. Deep down inside, I knew that I was gay.

My high school years were during the late 80s and being gay was dramatically different than it is today. The "gay" word had an even greater stigma attached to it. If you were associated with the word "gay," it often followed other words such as fairy, queer, effeminate, or fag. And, people who were openly gay were made fun of and stereotyped as musicians, interior designers, or hairstylists. Even the idea of "gays in the military" in the late 80s was an emerging topic. And, the military's "don't ask, don't tell" policy reinforced a narrative that kept me deep in the closet. As Catholic schools were notorious for instilling the fear of judgment, I had no plans of coming out as "gay" in high school.

Socially, I struggled to find which group I belonged to. On the one hand, I could hang with the "cool and popular" rich kids one day, while the next strike up a conversation with the kids we labeled "nerds and geeks." And, while I didn't fully connect with the other kids who were also on financial aid, I never made fun of them because I was in the same situation. While my friends talked about meeting girls and playing sports after school, I would just smile, but never partake in the conversation because I wasn't interested in either topic. In retrospect, I was never really part of one specific social group because I didn't seem to fit into any of them completely. It was as if I maintained the middle ground in high school. I fit in with everyone, and simultaneously, with no one. On the inside, I felt disconnected. I was hungry to find where I belonged and the group in which I could feel safe and comfortable just being myself.

Since this was the story running in the background, it

shouldn't be a surprise that for most of my high school years I felt ashamed, embarrassed, lost, confused, and afraid...to be authentically me.

COMING OUT OF THE CLOSET

You may have noticed that the title of this book is bold. The word "gay" is loaded and controversial. While some people have neutral feelings toward the word, others may have negative associations and feel discrimination related to it. Still others might feel proud and excited because the word represents their community or a part of their personal identity.

While this book is titled *Your Brand Should Be Gay (Even If You're Not)*, I want to be clear that this book is NOT about being "gay." In fact, you can be the most heterosexual, straitlaced, conservative person and you can still benefit from this book—just as long as you're interested in learning how branding can help you grow or expand your business.

So, as I've clearly mentioned: I am a gay man.

And I chose this title for two reasons.

First, it's my way of not hiding but overtly coming out of the closet. Regardless of what people may think about me, I'm still clear and confident about who I am. Through my own personal journey as a gay man, through the process of discovering who I truly was, I learned to accept who I am, make peace with it, and ultimately own it. If the word "gay" stops some people from reading this book, then it's their loss (not mine). Because this book contains years of branding insights that could alter the trajectory of their business.

Second, the title is a subtle way of demonstrating the power of a brand when it is not afraid to be fully expressed and authentic. Authentic branding stands out and captures our attention. Authentic branding elicits an emotional response from the market. Authentic branding compels us to take action (or not).

This book is *not* just another branding or marketing book.

This book is about Brand Authenticity.

Authenticity is about being real and genuine. It's about being yourself, owning it, and knowing that some people might reject you while others will embrace you. When it comes to building a business, an authentic brand is a declaration of who you are and who you're not. An authentic brand aligns your values, belief systems, and point of view with your products and services. When your brand is authentic, the people who connect with you—and buy from you—do so for the right reasons. More importantly, it's about the peace and comfort of knowing that it's OK. There's one thing I know for sure: when you're an authentic brand, you will be more successful, more profitable, and yes, more fulfilled.

HOW TO READ THIS BOOK

I'll warn you, as you read the teachings in this book, you'll never look at brands and branding the same way ever again. Read this book with an open mind and a hunger to learn something new. You will be challenged to dig deeper into your brand than ever before. You will be encouraged to be more creative and innovative. You'll appreciate both the art and science of branding.

Since the branding challenges you're facing as an entrepreneur or small-to-midsize business are different than those of the big firms, such as Starbucks, Nike, Apple, or Tiffany, I've included many stories—incorporating those from my own personal journey, and those of my clients to teach big concepts into practical application.

That said, I want you to learn how to *think* about branding (not just for your business as it stands today, but throughout its lifetime). I want you to be inspired by ideas within and outside your industry. You'll learn how to apply a methodology and process to take your business through a comprehensive and holistic approach to building an authentic brand. Ultimately, you'll embrace branding as a strategic lifestyle, and not as a fly-by-night tactic.

I want you to take full advantage of all the benefits of branding as a foundation for your business, because I believe branding has the power to change your business. And, branding has the power to change the world. Including yours.

The Foundation

CHAPTER ONE

The Truth about Branding

THE EIGHTEEN-KARAT-GOLD EARRINGS

A professor at the Kellogg School of Management asked a group of students how much they would pay for a pair of eighteen-karat-gold earrings. The students' average answer was $550. He asked a second group the same question except he qualified that the earrings were from Tiffany. The students' average answer increased by 60 percent to an astounding $873. He asked a third group of students how much they would pay for the same pair of earrings except this time he told them that the earrings were from Walmart. Surprisingly, the students' average answer decreased by 85 percent to a mere $81.[1]

---

1   Tim Calkins and Alice Tybout, Kellogg on Branding: The Marketing Faculty of Kellogg School of Management (New Jersey: John Wyley & Sons, 2005), 10.

What can you learn from this? Three things.

First, branding directly correlates to the price people are willing to pay for your product or service. Someone will spend according to their perception of the value of your products or services.

Second, while Tiffany and Walmart both have big businesses, their brands appeal to different target audiences. So, it's not that a bigger business commands a higher price. In fact, Tiffany appeals to a high-end target market. If they were to charge the same price as Walmart, their consumer would probably not find value in their brand and ultimately not purchase their products. Conversely, if Walmart charged the same price as Tiffany, they would have a challenging time moving products—if they were able to sell any products at all.

So, what do you think Tiffany's brand is ultimately appealing to?

Tiffany is selling an identity and status. Whereas, Walmart's brand appeals to price-point (i.e., the cheapest option). Their "Always Low Prices" slogan has reinforced this message for nineteen years.

Thirdly, it's important to understand the distinction between business and brand—and how the two should be inextricably linked. Simply put, your business refers to what you "make, do, or sell." That said, this next statement may be a difficult one for some of you to digest. No one cares about your business. They don't care about your offerings, whether it's a product, program, or service. It still surprises me that many entrepreneurs and business owners still lead by talking about the amazing features of their company and its offerings.

What do your target audiences care about?

They care about the *perception* of the value your business and offerings bring to them. Your brand is merely a translation of your business into an emotional connection between you and your target audiences. When you invest in building a brand the right way, you're bound to achieve business results more effectively and much faster than without a brand. You increase the likelihood of success in the process of launching, growing, and scaling your businesses. It's for these reasons that successful business owners and marketing teams invest in branding.

So, what *exactly* is a brand? Before we go any further, I need to clear up some potential confusion here at the beginning. Your brand is NOT:

- Marketing
- Advertising

- Public Relations
- Direct Response
- Social Media
- A Logo
- A Tagline/Slogan
- Your Colors
- Your Photographs
- Your Typography/Fonts
- Your Company or Product name
- Your Message
- And, last but not least, YOU

All of these are important and useful tools, tactics, and expressions to building a brand, but they are not your brand.

There are countless definitions of the word "brand" from many thought leaders that all have merit.

Seth Godin defines a brand as "the set of expectations, memories, stories, and relationships that, taken together, account for a consumer's decision to choose one product or service over another. If the consumer (whether it's a business, a buyer, a voter, or a donor) doesn't pay a premium, make a selection, or spread the word, then no brand value exists for that consumer."[2]

---

2   Seth Godin's Blog: https://seths.blog/2009/12/define-brand/.

Jeff Preston Bezos, founder of Amazon.com and one of the most quoted entrepreneurs in the world, defines a brand as "what other people say about you when you're not in the room."[3]

While there is no right or wrong definition of brand, I invite you to consider the definition that I've used in my career and that I learned from my first branding mentor, a pioneer and veteran in the Corporate Branding industry.

Brand is a *desired* perception.

If that's the case, then you don't own your brand. It resides in the minds of the people that you're communicating with. Therefore, *branding* is the process of creating, shaping, and influencing that desired perception in the marketplace.

It's that simple.

Many service providers in the branding industry do a superb job of over-complicating branding, using confusing industry jargon, or preaching about the importance and value of branding. But very rarely can they give you a simple definition of the word "brand." If someone can't define their terms, particularly the very industry that they're in, I'd think twice before working with them.

---

3   Inc.com: https://www.inc.com/bill-murphy-jr/17-jeff-bezos-quotes-that-suddenly-take-on-a-whole-new-meaning-after-2-stunning-decisions.html.

Let's explore a few examples to clarify the difference between business and brand:

	Business	Brand
Harley Davidson	Motorcycle Manufacturer	Delivering freedom on the open road and comradeship of a kindred spirit.
Nike	Footwear, Apparel, Equipment, Accessories	Bringing inspiration and innovation to every athlete.
Starbucks	Coffeehouse Chain	Inspiring and nurturing the human spirit—one person, one cup, and one neighborhood at a time.
Amazon	Technology company: e-commerce, cloud computing, digital streaming, artificial intelligence	Delivering the broadest selection of products and services at the lowest prices with minimal hassle.
BMW	Automobile and Motorcycle Manufacturer	The Ultimate Driving Machine

WHERE DOES BRANDING EXIST?

Let's try an exercise together.

Sit comfortably in a chair and put your dominant leg out in front of you. Take your dominant foot and rotate it in a clockwise direction. Continue circling your foot in a clockwise direction and with the pointer finger of your dominant hand, draw the number six in the air in front of you. As you draw the six, notice what happens to your foot. Has it moved a little bit counterclockwise? Did you make this move consciously?

Here's the science behind the phenomenon. You consciously turned your foot in a clockwise direction. Then when you drew the number six, you took the ability to do so from your subconscious. As you drew the six in midair, the subconscious took over the conscious. Consequently, your foot turned in the same direction that your finger moved when you drew the number. You have just witnessed the power of the subconscious.

What does the subconscious have to do with branding? Everything!

The formidable subconscious easily influences our conscious mind, and we don't even realize it. The most powerful way to build a brand is not in consumers' conscious minds but in their subconscious minds. Successful brands tap into the subconscious mind because, according to Harvard Business Review, 95 percent of all purchasing decisions are made in the subconscious.[4]

If you're trying to determine why people aren't buying from you, or you're working on how to influence the way people purchase from you, you need to stop focusing on

---

4   https://www.inc.com/logan-chierotti/harvard-professor-says-95-of-purchasing-decisions-are-subconscious.html.

their conscious activities and instead focus on the subconscious. Branding is the most powerful way to tap into their subconscious. While there are people who might do this unethically, I insist on approaching branding ethically and with integrity.

People who interact with your brand will decide in fifteen seconds whether or not they will buy from you. You have fifteen seconds or less to create an impression or perception. Their perception of your brand directly affects whether they will recommend you, follow you, listen to you, subscribe to your service, or complete whatever behavioral action you want them to take. Branding is about maximizing these fifteen seconds by tapping into the subconscious mind using the different visual, verbal, and behavioral cues to influence their perception.

As I've said, brand is a *desired* perception. I believe that in order to create this desired perception in the minds of others, you *first* need to have this same perception within your company and within yourself. While people come to us for a new brand, website, and logo, they usually get a dose of personal development as well. Often in the process, we transform people's mindsets by helping to illuminate and reveal who they truly are. You can have the ideal brand, but it starts with you. It starts with your mindset. Do you believe it yourself? Does it feel true to you? You need to be aligned with your brand.

I want you to wake up in the morning and know that you are aligned with your brand. I don't want you to question it. When you wake in the morning, do you question whether you are human or not? I want you to just have a knowing that you *are* your brand.

I often talk to entrepreneurs who sheepishly ask me to look at their logo or another aspect of their brand. It's evident that they are not proud of the brand that is supposed to represent their company. Sometimes they are embarrassed. When you know exactly who you are and who you are not, you show up as confident and proud of your brand. You're not trying to be someone that you're not, and you are not trying to be liked by everyone. If your goal is to be liked by everyone, you will inevitably suffer. Look at famous historical leaders for role models in this effort. Many were not concerned with being liked and stood for movements that were not popular with everyone. True confidence comes when you know that not everyone is going to agree with you, and you are OK with that. People with confidence naturally command attention and authority. They are an inspiration to others. We yearn for confidence because the underlying feeling is empowerment.

You can have a great logo, the best colors, and great messaging. You can have the right website and all of the marketing tools you need to portray a perception in the marketplace. You can have all of the right branding tools in place, but if the gap between who you *say* you are and who you *actually* are is wide, people will feel the disconnect created by your discomfort, just like they can see you wince when your shoes are too tight. You run the risk of hurting your credibility, compromising your brand, and compromising the degree to which people trust and respect you. At the end of the day, we do business with companies that we trust, like, and respect.

WHICH COMES FIRST: SALES, MARKETING, OR BRANDING?

If you're still on the fence about branding and you think that all this "touchy-feely" and "emotional" stuff isn't going to make a real difference in your business, keep reading. This section is especially for you.

I've heard it all before. I've had countless business owners tell me they don't need branding to grow their business. One group of people will argue that they just need to make more sales. Another group will tout better marketing as the solution to growth. Branding does inform marketing, but they are separate strategies. Marketing (along with direct-response, sales, advertising, social media, public relations) are designed to get our attention right now and elicit an immediate behavior. Branding, on the other hand, is not about grabbing your attention today. Instead, it's about creating a perception over time. And, the reason I always say that branding should come before marketing is because I often see companies use outlandish marketing tactics, gimmicks, and even neurolinguistic programming to trick people into buying from them. These tactics may generate revenue today, but they can tarnish a brand and negatively impact the overall customer lifetime value.

The beauty of entrepreneurs and small businesses is that they can be great at marrying branding and marketing to create unprecedented results. A lot of our clients understand marketing, so when we dial in their brand, they optimize their marketing strategies and tactics which result in better conversions and faster results. They are not just throwing guesswork against the wall and seeing what works. They are able to confidently say, "This is who we are. This is what we stand for. Love us or hate us." They take a proactive stance versus the reactive stance of marketing.

In short, we *need* marketing. It helps us make money. But you can make a lot more money and have a greater impact (while spending less on marketing and advertising) when you're clear on your brand.

So, what should you focus on—sales, marketing, or branding? I believe you need ALL three. But, where people get it wrong is they have the wrong context for branding. What I mean is that some people see branding as something to do *after* they make sales or *after* they implement their marketing. That's certainly one school of thought. And it has worked for many businesses in the past. But that doesn't mean it will continue to work today or in the very near future.

I'd like to broaden your context for branding, by relating it back to your business growth. Presumably, you're reading this branding book because that's one of the things you want. I'd argue there are three broad ways to grow your business.

THE OLD SCHOOL APPROACH: A "SALES-LED" COMPANY

In this approach, the CEO treats salespeople as the leaders who get all the glory, fame, and recognition. After all, they're the ones knocking down doors, dealing with rejection, and tirelessly chasing prospects in order to convert them into clients or customers. In this model, the CEO's underlying philosophy is to "sell, sell, sell"—and therefore, the business will grow. Historically, this approach has worked for many companies, but at its core there exists an "old school" mindset.

THE NEW SCHOOL APPROACH: A "MARKETING-LED" COMPANY

In this approach, it's not just the salespeople who are

responsible for the success or revenue of the company. In fact, it's now the marketing team who holds the purse strings. The marketing department gets more funding and attention. For a small business without an in-house marketing team, they turn to their marketing agency. They hand over thousands of dollars to help them qualify, target, and secure quality leads. In doing so, they help fill the pipeline for their sales team, supplying incoming leads for them to close. As you can see, this already seems a smarter way to grow your business. With this model, you're leveraging your time by focusing only on qualified leads. This approach works, and it's why it's considered the "new school" approach. It's why there are countless marketing agencies and consultants.

THE FUTURE: A "BRAND-LED" COMPANY

In a brand-led company, it's not just the burden of the sales or marketing teams to grow the business. Rather, the entire company, from the CEO to the receptionist, is unified and empowered around a singular Brand Purpose and Brand Promise (two concepts we'll get into later). In addition, the company's Brand Culture is now guided by a set of Brand Values that guide every behavior and set of actions that are "on-brand." And, more importantly, each and every employee lives the brand by internalizing: "How can I deliver on the brand?" Then expressing the answer through daily actions.

EVEN YOU KNOW IT'S TIME

There are obvious signs that a rebrand is in your future. If your company landscape has changed, for example, you may feel that is an obvious reason to rebrand. You might have a new mission or purpose. A shift in your most basic *raison d'etre* ("reason for being") definitely merits a rebranding conversation. For example, if you've been providing services and now want to focus exclusively on products, a rebrand is in order. You may have had a public relations disaster—or an actual one—and you're trying to distance yourself from it. In these cases, rebranding may help you achieve your goal. If you've managed to attract a new market—whether by choice or by accident—rebranding may make sense.

In the early 2000s, for example, Andersen Consulting split from its parent because its best clients wanted full consulting services, not just accounting. It rebranded as Accenture to further distance itself from the accounting giant (Good thing, too, as Andersen collapsed over its ties to Enron.). You may have new needs from existing customers like the Canadian arm of Radio Shack. After being bought out in a consumer electronics deal, they initially rebranded as The Source by Circuit City. But when its new owner began to falter, it became simply The Source—a move couldn't have had better timing. Circuits and radios are concepts from the past, and the new name suggests that no matter where electronics go in the future, The Source will be there to provide the needed tech (And both Circuit City and Radio Shack are now distant memories).

If you have new competition, rebranding might be in order. For example, to say things were different in the 90s than they were in the 50s is an understatement. Throughout those decades, Kentucky Fried Chicken had the word "fried" right there in its name. However, in 1991, we saw the change to KFC in a move away from that F-word. Too many healthy restaurants were giving the chicken giant a run for its money—so the move made sense.

While it's important to brand your business, don't do it for the wrong reason. For example, if all you've changed about your company is the management group—and the same business problems you've always had continue—rebranding will never work. Branding or rebranding will not solve the problems that have yet to be addressed by the new management itself.

You may think that it's time to consolidate all of your sub-brands under one flagship brand, but this might not be necessary, particularly if they have each built up brand equity of their own. Department store Macy's lost a staggering amount of brand equity when it moved to a "one-brand" policy and renamed iconic brands like Chicago's Marshall Field's and Memphis's Goldsmith's. Even at the time, the decision was seen as foolish; Macy's seemed to have recovered within the decade but is struggling once again.

If you've identified that you're having trouble connecting with your market, is that a branding problem? Or is it because your marketing is appalling, your customer service is poor, or your services aren't delivered well? You need to answer this question honestly. Be careful—not every issue is one that branding can solve.

Branding can dramatically increase sales, which is, of course, a great result. However, if your business doesn't have the infrastructure to handle the increase in business, then branding can have a detrimental effect. A successful brand will quickly deteriorate if customer satisfaction erodes. If you can't handle the burden of increased fulfillment, then branding will quickly do you more harm than good.

If you're selling a commodity, great branding might not help. Commodities are items such as natural resources: sugar, steel, gasoline. Do you really care what brand your gas is, or do you simply care which station offers a lower price?

Finally, and this is a major one for entrepreneurs and small businesses, if you or your team are inadequate in the sales process, branding can't help you solve your "sales" problem. While branding can "pre-sell" your products or services and help people want your product or service without a "hard sell," there is no substitute for sales. If you are uncomfortable with a sales conversation, or uncomfortable asking for money, then branding isn't going to solve your problems. A great brand will get you more conversations and make these conversations easier, but it won't ever replace sales as a necessary business activity.

PERSONAL BRANDING VERSUS COMPANY BRANDING

One of the top three questions I get asked is whether or not a business owner should build a Personal Brand or Company Brand. For several years, I've resisted the term "Personal Branding" because the advice that I've seen from self-proclaimed "Personal Branding Experts" was either poor and ineffective or simply recommendations to boost people's egos without any consideration for whether the resulting image was authentic or not.

It's a topic I have to address because even to this day, I am asked if I'm in the business of Personal Branding (since the word "People" is in my company name). In answer to this question, I explain that my company's goal is to help companies create a brand that people love—particularly their target customers or clients, ideal employees and strategic partners, and other stakeholders who engage with their brand. As such, our company focuses on building Company Brands (it just so happened that several of the companies I've branded have big personalities as the front-facing CEO or thought leader).

It's also a topic worth explaining because it's a term the market has embraced. I've learned to embrace it as a discipline because of two driving forces. First, social media has proven that Personal Brands can have a massive impact and influence in the marketplace—whether it's in promoting a political agenda, kickstarting a social movement, or even endorsing a company's product or service. Secondly, there are some legitimate Personal Branding experts with real-world experience and strategic insights, plus methods for using Personal Branding to build businesses. I've gained appreciation and respect of Personal Branding, as a discipline, because of them.

So, here's my view on the differences between Personal Branding and Company Branding (in the context of business building):

- Personal Branding involves creating a business, enterprise, or organization that is centered around a singular person (usually the founder or CEO, but not always). The personality or ethos of the front-facing person is what people buy into.
- Company Branding involves creating a business, enterprise, or organization that is centered around the collective group of people who are fulfilling on the same purpose and vision, and who share the same set of values, beliefs, and operating principles. In this case, the ethos of the Company Brand is what people buy into.

As with every aspect of branding, there are pros and cons to building a Personal Brand over a Company Brand. For example, if you're publishing a book or trying to get speaking gigs, a Personal Brand can help you. If you're a service provider with a unique set of experiences, skills, or wisdom, a Personal Brand can help you too. However, if you loathe the spotlight or your personal past experience could hurt the perception of the business overall, you may want to downplay your Personal Brand. Additionally, if you want to build and scale a business to sell it, building a Personal Brand is not the smartest move (it's harder to sell a business based on a Personal Brand).

TO BRAND OR NOT TO BRAND?

If you've mastered your sales process and marketing campaigns, but your business isn't where you want it to be, or you're not sure how to take your business growth to the next level, chances are you need to brand. When companies are looking to brand or rebrand, they frequently share one of these familiar phrases:

- "We don't like our logo."
- "Our website needs updating or is outdated."
- "Our branding is inconsistent, from our website to our social media."
- "We're ashamed of our brand. We usually tell people not to judge us for our branding."

- "Our branding doesn't accurately represent who we are or where we're going."
- "We can't justify or command premium pricing."
- "We're not converting as well as we used to."
- "We don't have the right message. We're not saying the right things."
- "We don't know how to articulate who we are in a concise sentence or two."

So, usually, there's a frustration that the brand is not where it should be or the company has a strong desire to make the brand better. But I see these frustrations and desires as symptoms of a larger problem—a lack of *authenticity* in the brand. And similar to a holistic doctor that likes to get to the source of the disease, rather than a more traditional Western doctor that gives you medication to appease the symptoms, I don't like to treat the symptoms. I like to get to the source of the problem. You see, there are countless companies who can design your logo, update your website, or make your designs look better than they are today. I don't stop there. I want you to get to the root of the problem. I want you to look at how the brand can become more authentic.

WHAT IS YOUR PROBLEM?

Every business and every brand should solve a problem for their client or customer. Branding can also solve *your* problems as a business owner or marketing team. To paraphrase Charles Kettering, the famed inventor and head of research for GM, a problem well-defined is a problem half-solved. Before you begin branding, let's determine the problem (or problems) you're trying to solve. With this end in mind, I always ask my clients, "*why* do you want to build a brand?" Sometimes, the answer is simply "because I don't have one."

Well, I'd argue that "not having a brand" isn't a good enough reason to invest in branding—especially when you're working with an agency. It's like asking someone why you want children or why you want a puppy—and your answer is "because I don't have one." Just because you don't have one doesn't mean you should have one. I believe everyone can benefit from branding, but not everyone is *ready* for branding. Branding takes time. Branding is deep work. And, your brand is something you will continue to nurture and evolve over time.

To keep things real and tangible, ask yourself these two practical questions:

1. What is (are) the business problem(s) you're looking to solve through branding?
2. What is (are) the brand problem(s) you're trying to solve through branding?

These questions represent opposite sides of the same coin. The truth is that business problems are branding problems. When executed properly, branding can solve many of your business problems. My intention is to provide you with the insights and tools to solve *your* branding problems.

Your branding problems can be solved by identifying where your brand lacks authenticity. Let me take you on a behind-the-scenes journey to learn how some companies transformed their brands from embarrassingly inauthentic to unapologetically authentic.

CHAPTER TWO

The Case for Authentic Brands

YOU'RE SELLING UP MARKET, BUT YOUR BRAND IS DOWN MARKET

Several years ago, I met the head of a high-end consulting company at a business event we were both sponsoring. I'd heard of him, as we had mutual friends and clients, so I genuinely wanted to learn more about his company. I approached his booth, introduced myself, and said, "Hey, tell me about the company and how it works."

I stood there for several minutes and listened to his pitch. It sounded like a great service, something that I could even use myself. But something felt off, and at first glance, I couldn't quite figure out what it was. When he was done, I said, "That sounds cool. Thank you." Instead of asking for more information, I said my goodbyes and turned to walk to the next company's display. Before I could take two steps, he stopped me.

"Wait! Before you go. Can I please ask you a question? You're our ideal target audience. I'm curious why you didn't go for our service?" he asked.

Since he asked, I felt obliged to give him my feedback. I paused and scanned the poorly assembled branding showcased in his trade show booth. The clip art images on his marketing collateral seemed to be mass-produced by a junior graphics production artist (at best). I looked back at him and pegged his rumpled T-shirt and blue jeans as brands from either TJ Maxx or H&M. Even from a few feet away, I could see the service price list and this company's service was five times that of its closest competitor. Verbally he had shared that his service would result in a state-of-the-art high-quality deliverable, but the rest of his brand left me with doubts.

I replied, "Well, you're selling 'up market,' but your brand is 'down market.'" I had heard that this particular person loved brutal honesty, so telling him my unfiltered thoughts would be received as a gift.

And, it hit him like a ton of bricks. He understood immediately.

His company's message was clear, but his branding was off

base. It was inauthentic. He and his branding didn't "look the part," especially for someone like me. And, since I was the ideal target audience, I explained that I wouldn't hire his company, based on his branding. Because my brand was important to me, I hire other brands that align with mine. I'm looking for "sophisticated and premium," not cheap and mass market.

The moral of the story is that when a brand is inauthentic, people consciously or subconsciously hesitate to buy. And unless you work exceedingly hard to convince them otherwise, those people generally won't buy in the long run.

That said, I always tell people that authenticity can't be bought. I can't make a company authentic. I can, however, show a company how to *be* more authentic.

HOW MUCH SHOULD YOU SPEND ON MARKETING VERSUS BRANDING?

To answer the question of marketing spend versus branding spend, I invite you to understand a common term that's used at the big brand consultancies—it's called Brand Value. Interbrand, one of the pioneers in measuring Brand Value, defines it as "the Net Present Value (NPV) or today's value of the earnings the brand is expected to generate in the future."

This valuation approach is borrowed from the same corporate theory and practice of how business and financial assets are valued. Without going into too much detail, there are three key elements to this complex formula: financial forecasting, role of branding, and brand strength.

According to Forbes, Microsoft and Apple both have high Brand Value. You could probably guess that Apple has a higher Brand Value. The story gets interesting when we find out that their ad spend, *as a percentage of their total Brand Value*, is relatively low. It gets even more interesting when we discover just how low it is for each company, with Microsoft at 2.5 percent and Apple 1.1 percent. Apple spends 1.1 percent to get almost double the Brand Value.[5]

The takeaway of this story is this: When you invest in building a brand, you maximize your marketing spend, because your brand continues to do the work for you, even after your marketing campaigns are completed. Not only will you improve the efficacy of your marketing efforts, but you may end up spending less on your marketing efforts than your competitors without a brand or who have a weaker brand.

But, here's the deal. You still need to spend money on marketing. To properly answer the question of *how much* to spend between marketing and branding, I recommend establishing a few guidelines.

---

5   Jason Green and Mark Henneman, Optimizing Growth: Predictable and Profitable Strategies to Understand Demand and Outsmart Your Competitors (New Jersey: John Wiley & Sons, 2018), 133.

First, commit to creating a budget, with a percentage of revenue allocated for branding and marketing individually. Depending on your access to capital, growth trajectory, and risk tolerance, these percentages may vary. From experience, I generally see a range of 5-7 percent for branding and 20-50 percent for marketing. For example:

- $1,000,000 revenue
- Five percent of revenue = $50,000 branding budget
- Twenty percent of revenue = $200,000 marketing budget

Second, adjust those percentages and budget, based on the strength of your brand and the stage of your business. Following is a chart for illustrative purposes to help you plan your budget.

Brand Strength	Business Stage	Branding Budget	% of Revenue	Marketing Budget	% of Revenue
Nonexistent	Starting	Low	5%	Low	20%
Average	Growing	High	7%	High	40%
Strong	Scaling	Low	5%	High	50%
Average	Stabilizing	Average	6%	Low	20%

Our Apple and Microsoft example shows that the investment in branding can be quantified, and the budgeting chart suggests how you can fund this type of result for your business. Your branding and marketing spend should be tailored to your current brand strength and your present business stage. My suggested percentages assume that you're looking to invest in branding to improve the performance of your business and amplify your company's marketing and sales efforts.

BRAND AUTHENTICITY: THE METRIC FOR SUCCESS

Now that we got logistics and economics out of the way, I'd like to redefine how to measure the success of a brand.

This may be a hard conversation for some of you. Why? Because many marketing agencies and business experts have taught the masses to believe that a "successful" brand is defined in terms of likes, followers...or even top-line sales.

I believe that the success of your brand has nothing to do with any of these. Likes and followers may make you feel good, but whether you're building a legacy business or scaling a business to sell, they don't truly matter in the long run. Don't misunderstand me. You need marketing. You need the tactics that build an audience and help you acquire leads. And, you need to make sales if you want to be in business.

But, while marketing helps you eat, branding helps you sleep.

The businesses that get it right treat their brand as an

investment. Too many entrepreneurs and business owners are just out to make a buck, regardless of whether their products or services actually make an impact on people. They're looking for overnight success but are unwilling to do the work to create value in the marketplace. It happens all too often and it's a shame.

The real secret to building a successful brand is authenticity.

The authenticity of your brand is far more important than a one-time customer or client. Because we buy—and will continue to buy—from brands that earn our respect and trust because they're genuine and real. We buy from brands that don't manipulate us or trick us into purchasing something we don't need or want. We buy from brands that actually solve our problems. And more and more, we buy from brands that make our lives just a little better...sometimes even transforming them.

Now that you understand the impact of an authentic brand, the budgeting logistics, and how to measure your brand's success, we need to address the critical precursor to branding success—your mindset.

A solid brand will take your company to new heights. However, you'll get the most bang for your buck from your branding budget when you don't underestimate the importance of having an empowering mindset.

CHAPTER THREE

Building an Empowering Branding Mindset

"I WANT X, BUT Y"

The way I looked at goals changed when I attended my first Landmark Education event. At the time, I was in my twenties in a full-time, salaried position in a different industry in which I was successful, but unfulfilled and unchallenged. I knew that I needed to get out of the job I was in and move on, but I felt stuck. I couldn't take the steps needed to find a new position because I was held back by fear. One of the most powerful thought tools I learned at the event to break through this fear mentality was "I want X, but Y."

Here's how it works: Fill in "X" with what you want and "Y" with the excuse you're using for not getting "X." When I was taught this process, I thought, "Cool, I like games. I'll play."

So, I replaced "X" with "to quit my job" and replaced "Y" with "I don't have another job lined up." Strung together, the statement read: "I want to quit my job, but I don't have another job lined up." I wasn't an entrepreneur at the time and had only ever worked for someone else, so my belief system told me that I needed to have a job, because how else was I going to pay my rent, cover my car payment, pay for clothes, and afford entertainment? Clearly, I was in the "employee" mindset at the time.

The next step in using this tool is to ask, "What does 'Y' mean to me?" In this case, my question was, "What does not having another job lined up mean to me?" In other words, what is the *story* or meaning I am giving it? I answered the question by saying, "Well, I wouldn't be able to survive because I wouldn't be able to pay my bills. I wouldn't be able to do the things that I enjoy because they require money. I would be perceived as a failure or irresponsible." I continued to drill down these thoughts until I came up with the true "Y." Deep down, I felt that I would not be *in control* of my life. So, I rephrased the formula, replacing the "X" and "Y", and wrote, "I want to quit my job, but I would lose control of my life."

Huh? What was I talking about?

When I reread that statement, I realized how ridiculous it was. I didn't choose to venture out on my own at this time, but if I had, I'd actually be taking control of my life. I wouldn't be relying on a company to remain stable in order to pay my salary each month. Instead, I would be relying on my own creativity, ingenuity, and skills to generate income each month. Ultimately that change would put me in legitimate control rather than false perceived control. Even if I chose to look for a new position, I would be in control because *I* would choose which job to accept. Either way, I would give myself even more control and autonomy.

This reframing and realization was a game-changer for me. I had deluded myself into not quitting my job because I falsely believed that I would be out of control when the result would actually be quite the opposite.

The very next day, I put in my two weeks' notice. It felt great to resign with dignity and integrity. I made it very clear that I would be changing industries and that I had no desire to go after the company's clients. Leaving in good standing allowed me to retain my relationship with the company and my former clients, and even lead to a high-level position with one of the company's clients later down the road. This new role serendipitously led me into the branding industry. I was asked to head up a Brand Culture division at a boutique brand consulting firm in New York City.

Ultimately this next role really put me in control of my own life. I landed a big account for my new firm, and within months of resigning from the other company, I was in a new field, consulting with an international biosciences company, and traveling all across Europe and South America. And, even during an economic recession, I was making more money than my previous salaried position. Imagine if I had let my false belief keep me in the old position where I wasn't going anywhere?

We've all been there. Anyone who has tried to lose weight catches themselves thinking, "it might work for others, but it won't work for me." It can be difficult to look at a process and imagine the end result. Even as entrepreneurs and small business owners, we allow our false beliefs to hold us back (often in regard to the challenges that will make the biggest difference for our companies) from committing to branding. Ironically, the very reasons a company resists branding, are often the very reasons that they need it. They may think they don't want to spend money on branding, but little do they know that an initial investment will translate into a greater profit down the road. They may not want to take the time to brand, but ultimately, branding will save them time and energy in the long run. When companies invest time and money in branding, they see savings in their marketing budget, their sales budget, and multiple places throughout their company.

That said, I get it. Branding is abstract. It's not within your comfort zone. I understand that it might feel scary or intimidating to embark upon. I want you to know that I've heard it all before, and you're not alone. In my experience, there are usually five reasons that companies don't invest in branding. All of these reasons are mindset-related. Overcoming these barriers requires a complete mindset shift before you can truly experience the full power of branding.

Let's unpack all five mindset shifts.

MINDSET SHIFT #1: BRANDING IS INTANGIBLE, BUT ITS BENEFITS ARE TANGIBLE

As mentioned previously, many companies don't take advantage of branding because they don't understand what a brand is. I think companies fall into one of two camps. It may seem obvious, but either the company is aware of branding and its power, or it doesn't know about or understand branding at all.

The first camp includes companies that don't realize branding is its own business practice. If they hear the word "branding," they assume it is synonymous with marketing. Usually, these companies are smaller and have been around for years.

Most entrepreneurs fall into the second camp. The word "brand" comes up frequently in entrepreneurial conversations, and branding is a popular topic in the blogs and publications entrepreneurs read. The correct definition still eludes this camp sometimes. These entrepreneurs know that they need branding, but they don't know why. They don't know how it can benefit their company, and they don't know how to start the process.

These companies need to learn about the tangible benefits of branding. Understanding the tangible benefits gives a company a goal and a target outcome.

As evidenced in big brands and from many of my clients over the years, branding helps companies create a unique perception in people's minds, and emotional connection with their target audiences, and impacts the company's bottom line. More explicitly, branding helps them make more money—either by attracting more qualified clients or by allowing them to increase their fees, consequently improving their profitability. Branding also helps them increase their conversion rates. Finally, branding exposes clients to new opportunities, whether a media interview, joint business venture, or even a strategic alliance.

In short, when you go through the branding process, it has a tangible impact on your bottom line, which is what business owners are looking for.

MINDSET SHIFT #2: BRANDING IS A REVENUE-GENERATING INVESTMENT, NOT A LIABILITY COST

Companies are often reluctant to commit funds for branding because they don't place importance on branding. When you look at where your company is currently spending money, you can see what is considered important or a company priority. The choice not to allocate money to branding is rarely driven by a true lack of funds. If branding were considered important, you would find a way to allocate money for it. Just think, if you developed a life-threatening disease, you would figure out how to cover the expensive medical treatment required. Or if a loved one were kidnapped, and a demand came for twenty thousand dollars to be paid tomorrow, you can't tell me that you wouldn't come up with the money. You would find a way because your health and your loved one are important to you. Branding isn't a matter of life or death, but it is a key element to your company's success.

That said, building on Mindset Shift #1, in which branding has a direct correlation to tangible benefits, Mindset #2 is about relating to branding as an investment into your future, not a cost or expense. Every year, I recommend that you allocate a set budget to invest in building your brand—the same as you would for your marketing, advertising, and sales needs. Investment in branding is an investment in your company's future health.

MINDSET SHIFT #3: BRANDING HAPPENS OVER TIME, NOT OVERNIGHT

When it comes to time, the mindset issues are similar to money. Often companies don't make the time because they don't understand the importance of branding. They are not planning ahead and end up with a reactive approach to branding. They only pay attention to their brand when they need to respond to problems such as a publicity nightmare, low sales, declining conversions, or even a hacked website. Problems come later when they think, "Let's work on our brand." Unfortunately, there is no line item for this work in the budget, and the time has not been allocated. They have not thought, "Every year we need to spend 'X' amount of time on building our brand."

Most companies don't know how long branding takes. The truth is that branding isn't a "one and done" type of activity. Branding does not create an "overnight sensation." As the saying goes, "Rome wasn't built in a day." Similarly, a brand is not built overnight. And it certainly isn't built just because you have a logo. When you embark on branding, it's a long-term investment. It is a lifestyle choice because it influences all future decisions.

I think it's also important to properly address the question of "how much time to allocate" to branding. The answer lies with your priorities. Identify which part of your business needs the most help, and this will point to which aspect of branding you could most benefit from. Personally, I believe all facets of branding are important, but some aspects are not as time sensitive as others. For example, you might find that your messaging may be more important than updating your logo or social media pages in order to increase sales right now. Or, you might find that your website needs a revamp because most of your business is conducted online and your marketing efforts are negatively impacted. The solution to the question of time is identifying and working on the top priorities now and being prepared to work on the others over time.

MINDSET SHIFT #4: THE INTANGIBLE BENEFITS OF BRANDING EXCEED THE TANGIBLE BENEFITS

In the twentieth century, Paul Ekman identified six basic emotions (anger, disgust, fear, happiness, sadness, and surprise) and Robert Plutchik identified eight, which he grouped into four pairs of polar opposites (joy-sadness, anger-fear, trust-distrust, surprise-anticipation).[6] It has been said that these basic emotions are innate and universal, automatic, and fast. They trigger behavior that achieves a high survival value.

When we think about branding in relation to this school of psychology, we see two distinct parallels. The first one is

---

6   https://www.google.com/amp/s/www.psychologytoday.com/us/blog/hide-and-seek/201601/
    what-are-basic-emotions%3famp.

that branding is a "survival mechanism" for a business—branding helps a business survive in a competitive business landscape. Most companies engage a branding agency because they are in crisis mode. They're reacting to something that isn't working in their business—perhaps their revenue is low, or their reputation is being threatened. The second parallel is a bit more intangible. Whenever a company goes through a comprehensive and thorough branding process, their entire energetic and emotional state transforms. The company's employees become happier, more excited, more confident, and prouder of their business than ever before. I've never met anyone whose new brand put them in an emotional state of fear, anxiety, anger, or hatred.

One of the biggest mindset shifts is a realization that the intangible benefits far exceed the tangible benefits—because ultimately, they also become the driving force behind the tangible benefits. Think of it this way: We all know that money itself doesn't make us happy (if you think it does, you might be fooling yourself). But what makes us happy are all the things we're able to do as a result of having money—whether it's creating the experiences we want to have, supporting the important people in our lives, and improving (or even transforming) the way we live our lives.

When your brand empowers you with more confidence, pride, and happiness, don't you think you will show up differently when talking with prospects or clients? I don't just think so, I've witnessed it. And this heightened energetic state attracts more clients and customers, more revenue, and more opportunities.

Furthermore, consistent with Abraham Maslow's hierarchy of needs, I've found that my clients appreciate their brand for reasons beyond survival or security needs. Rather, their brand elevates their status. They gain more respect, recognition, and self-actualization. If a founder has built a company hoping that it will bring personal happiness through respect and recognition, an authentic brand will ultimately bring this happiness into his or her life.

MINDSET SHIFT #5: BRANDING ONLY WORKS WHEN YOU TRUST THE PROCESS

Trust is the most important mindset shift of the five. The most serious problem related to trust happens when the company doesn't trust the agency, designer, or branding professional that they have hired. Obviously, if you don't trust an agency, you shouldn't hire them, but it can be more complicated than that. Many companies do not know what to look for in a trusted branding partner. They might hire a branding partner only to realize halfway through the project that they aren't delivering as they promised.

Often, the founder or employees involved in the branding work don't trust that the process will work because it seems so abstract. While the process is deep and holistic, it is not as predictable as knowing that "if we do 'this,' then we get 'that.'"

When you are baking, you add various ingredients together that might actually taste terrible on their own. The combination of thoroughly mixing these ingredients and the addition of both heat and time results in a cake. Seeing the individual raw ingredients on the kitchen counter doesn't instill trust that the result will be something edible or even delicious. Branding is even less linear than baking, and people trust best when they see a linear progression. It is true, however, that if you engage in branding, you see better results in your marketing, sales, and internal company culture. The results just don't appear as the outcome of a simple $A + B = C$ equation.

Companies might not trust that branding will work for their business, as if their company is unique and different, and they don't need it. Just like with weight loss, you might assume that the particular needs and idiosyncrasies of your company won't allow branding to work for you. Companies get so caught up in their own internal problems that they can't imagine there is such a straight-forward solution out there.

Branding deals with the realm of perception, and people often don't trust what they can't see. While you can't see perception, it is still very real. People have perceptions all day long. Branding just brings what is in the subconscious into the conscious. People don't trust it because they can't see it or touch it.

I have plenty of examples to share with you of brands that pull their weight and really support their companies. Unfortunately, you're probably all too familiar with those brands that don't serve their companies because you've been on the receiving end of their misalignment. Usually it becomes real for you when something in the business isn't working, or it's not working as well as you'd like it to and you can't put your finger on the source of the problem.

Let's look at the top five branding problems that I've seen over the past decade. More accurately, these are areas where your brand is "inauthentic." Inauthenticity is the true root of the problem.

Signs of an Inauthentic Brand

CHAPTER FOUR

An Inauthentic Name

NAMING IS A CREATIVE PROCESS

Naming your company can be one of the most difficult and challenging tasks. It's the equivalent to naming a baby. And just like you, we (branding professionals) have the same challenges naming our own companies.

In the fall of 2010, I was living in New York City. I had just gone through the personal relationship breakup I mentioned in the Introduction, resigned from one of the top brand consulting firms in Dubai, attended a spiritual retreat, and embarked on a quest to determine the next chapter in my life. All of which led me to start my own branding company. At this point, I was faced with the same challenge every entrepreneur and business owner faces—what to call the company.

I started by reviewing all of my thoughts about what I

wanted the company to represent. What it stood for. How it would be different. I examined my vision for the agency. Surely, I thought, looking in that direction would lead me to a name that I would love. My vision was to bring a holistic, Fortune 500-level branding approach to entrepreneurs and small to midsize businesses who were at the source of making an impact on people.

I used my journal to capture my ideas for a company name. The initial round of results generated several horrible names, and the best one of the lot was "360° Brand Source." I thought, well, 360° would represent "holistic" and "Source" would represent the idea that the brand is the inspiration and central driving force of the business. And, as you probably know it's difficult to find an available domain/URL (either in use or parked for sale). The 360BrandSource.com URL was available, and I thought this should be my name! But, despite the domain's availability, the 360° Brand Source name was a complete flop for several reasons. No one was excited about the name. It didn't meet the three main requirements of a name: It didn't evoke emotion. It was difficult to remember (and the number one branding criteria for a solid name is "memorability"). It didn't tell a story. Plus, it didn't roll off the tongue. Defeated, I went back to the drawing board and decided to continue the naming process.

As I was currently unemployed, I spent much of my time

journaling, reading, and meditating. I also turned to yoga. Practicing four to five times a week, I became really good at Ashtanga and Vinyasa. I recall my friend asking me one day if I ever practiced Bikram or hot yoga. I hadn't. She said I should check out this yoga studio in Brooklyn called "Yoga to the People." As a creature of habit, I never did, but I filed that information in the back of my mind. I didn't know it at the time, but it was bound to resurface into my awareness.

A few months later, I was visiting family in Northern California. I went to the local Equinox Fitness Club in San Francisco to work out and take a yoga class. Afterward, I found myself at a nearby restaurant for lunch. I started to journal about my day and capture more ideas I had for starting my own business. When my food arrived, I put my pen down and looked up at the signs and writings on the restaurant wall. I saw a neon-lit sign that said, "Feed the People." In that moment I pondered: *What about Branding For The People?*

I loved it immediately, and countless ideas raced through my mind as to what I would do with a branding company under that name. Anxious on account of past domain name disappointments, I pulled out my iPhone to see if brandingforthepeople.com was available.

It was! Needless to say, I grabbed it. And at the low price tag of $4.99. Little did I know that $4.99 would generate millions of dollars for me over the next several years.

I think it's worth noting that when it comes to starting a business—and even naming it—sometimes you have to clarify your vision while simultaneously allowing the universe to send you guiding messages and ideas. Sometimes, we just need to be present to the conversations and moments that surround us. If it weren't for yoga, or my friend's recommendation, or my lunch in San Francisco, I probably would not have the name Branding For The People. After a failed name and additional brainstorming on names, the name came to me serendipitously.

What happens if you don't ultimately get the same messages or inspiration in your naming process. Or, what if you're not a natural creative, right-brain thinker and the brainstorming process is difficult? Or, what if you know you need to change an existing name for your established business, but you're not sure where to start? If either of these scenarios applies, then going through a naming process may be in order. Whether you decide to brainstorm names on your own or hire a branding partner, investing the time to come up with the perfect name can save you time *and* money down the road (more on this process at the end of the chapter).

IS YOUR NAME MISLEADING?

Gregory Serdahl, the CEO of Massage America, was one of my first clients when I started consulting on my own in New

York City. When I met Gregory, he was offering a "2-for-1" special on massages. Since I love massages, I took him up on his offer. Eventually, we got to talking about his business. He had been running a successful business for over a decade serving the New York City market, particularly local gyms that gave him access to professional athletes and corporate executives. However, he expressed that he wanted to go through a rebrand. I was thrilled because I now had the opportunity to work on a brand that offered services that I believe in—a big departure from the Fortune 500 brands I used to work with.

We met at my co-working space one morning, and I began my line of questioning.

"How many locations do you have throughout America?" I asked.

"Just the one in Union Square in Manhattan," Gregory replied.

"Got it. And is massage the *only* service you provide?" I continued.

Gregory nonchalantly responded, "Actually, we offer a wide range of therapeutic massage services, but also wellness programs like acupuncture and yoga, plus nutrition counseling." This suite of offerings made perfect sense, as I had already observed Gregory to be a deeply Zen and spiritual human being.

With a slightly puzzled look on my face, I posed a question no one had ever asked him, "Then *why* is your company called 'Massage America'—when you provide more than massage services, and you occupy only one location in Manhattan?"

I shared that the "Massage America" name was completely inauthentic because it was misleading and borderline deceptive. Needless to say, after he realized what seemed so obvious to me, he committed to change the name. His new name eventually required an entirely new brand. While he knew a rebrand would require an investment, he could see that his name was the cause of many lost opportunities.

Several weeks later, I recommended "Mpower Bodywork." This new name played on the word "empower" since his services "empower" his clients. In addition, the term "bodywork" served as an umbrella underneath which he could organize all of his massage, wellness, and nutrition services. Luckily the website domain was available, marking the rebirth of Massage America.

Today, Gregory continues to operate under the name Mpower Bodywork, and his business has seen unprecedented growth. According to Gregory, "Massage America had gone through many changes over a fifteen-year period, and we had lost our identity and core values. For us, branding was a process of distillation: looking at what we were currently doing best and remembering 'the why' that was driving our business in the beginning. All of that culminated in a new name, Mpower Bodywork, and a new Visual Identity that accurately reflects our core values and allows us more room and clear direction for new growth."

IS YOUR NAME LOCATION-SPECIFIC?

Craig Handley, the co-founder of ListenUp Español, a multimillion-dollar call center located in the United States and Mexico, wanted to expand the business in the US and move outside the Spanish-speaking market. While the company can provide both English and Spanish-speaking call center representatives, American companies regularly dismissed them as an option because their name gives the impression that they only serve the Spanish-speaking market.

Like many multi- or international companies, a brand name must be able to successfully cross borders and translate to different markets. Failure to do so can curtail business growth. ListenUp Español was not interested in letting a name hinder their fast growth trajectory. They tasked my firm with the rebranding and renaming of the company.

After a series of strategy and naming sessions, we finally

arrived at ListenTrust. This name leveraged the word "listen" from their original name, but also conveyed a benefit-oriented feature, i.e., "trust," that could appeal to both their current clientele who need Spanish-speaking call center representatives, as well as new clients who want English-speaking call center representatives.

In addition to its broadness and geographic neutrality, the new name helped them tell a better brand story. That is, ListenTrust makes a human connection. Why? Because the company is masterful at *listening* to its clients' customers and earning their *trust*, and in the process, improving their clients' business. The entire team loved the name and voted for it unanimously.

Craig Handley commented shortly after our work together: "Rebranding can be a pain-in-the-ass process, and it can be difficult for a company to let go of their old brand. Our employees and industry love our new brand and the story behind it. The new brand opens up more markets for us to sell into and really gives us the bigger company image for us to fulfill our vision for growth. It's very empowering when you have the right name and story to go with it."

IS YOUR NAME ATTRACTING THE WRONG PEOPLE?

Sue Thompson approached me with a desire to rebrand her company because she felt her branding wasn't aligned between her two entities: Abundance Accounting and The Mastery of Money. I asked her two questions that would ultimately lead us down the right path to rename and rebrand her accounting firm. The first question was the same one I asked Gregory Serdhal of Massage America: "Are accounting services all that you provide?"

Sue responded, "No, we also provide controller-type services, business consulting, business coaching, wealth creation consulting, and even payroll."

In our discussions, I learned that accounting was just the entry point for her clients to gain access to her true genius and the full value of what her company provides. In essence, Sue is an expert in helping business owners achieve their lifestyle goals. I told her that neither business name would give the perception of the full range of her services. And although "abundance" is a powerful word, it was not attracting her ideal target audiences.

Then I asked her: "Who are your ideal target audiences?"

After listening intently, she confessed that she really preferred to work with clients who were a bit more established and who found value in her higher-end services (not just accounting or bookkeeping). As a side note, she admitted that her services were historically and primarily part of a male-dominated industry, particularly where she lived in Montana. This insight prompted me to admit that her branding had more of a "feminine" energy and feel to it. And it looked and sounded too "woo-woo" (a term that can be seen as a derogatory term relating to spirituality, mysticism, or alternative medicine). Sue was fine with woo-woo, because she is a very spiritual person. But, highlighting this aspect of her as a dominant part of her brand wouldn't do any favors for her business.

Through a complete brand strategy process and several rounds of naming, we agreed to retire the two existing names and merge them into one new name: "The CFO Agency." The rationale for the new name was based on two key factors:

1. CFO, or Chief Financial Officer, is a C-Suite Executive title that would immediately convey a higher stature of services.
2. "Agency" would be a unique appendage compared to other similar companies in the industry that used "Firm," "LLC," or "& Partners" to signal a corporation with a team of people.

Shortly after the name change and rebrand, Sue claimed, "The branding process allowed us to reposition in the marketplace. The new name and brand clarified our company's services and added the emotional component so it made it easier for clients to say 'Yes.' Naturally, revenues increased because people are happy to pay a premium when they understand the value that they are receiving."

IS YOUR NAME TOO ABSTRACT?

Daniel Hyman is an energy/lightworker. Some people may refer to him as a Shaman. At its core, Daniel helps people create more love in their life, which in turn creates better results in other aspects of their lives as well as overall greater results and fulfillment. The very nature of Daniel's work is abstract, ethereal, and definitely "woo-woo" to the majority of people. However, he believes in his work with all of his soul and is committed to making his work more accessible to the masses.

Daniel and I met in Arizona at an event, in which I was a speaker and a sponsor. From a distance, I could see Daniel checking out our booth, but for the majority of the event, he avoided coming over. Eventually, Daniel approached me. He started by telling me that he had avoided meeting me because he had already spent over $100,000 on branding with another branding firm. He was worried that by even talking to me, he would open the flood gates and have to spend even more money.

He complained about his previous branding firm for about ten minutes. He wasn't completely happy and still needed some help. "Rather than spending more money on the 'branding' part," he said, "can you just help redesign some presentations and workbooks for my company, EarthStar18?"

He was asking me the wrong question. He should have asked, "Do you think my brand name, EarthStar18, will help me bring my work to the masses?"

But, of course, most entrepreneurs don't know what they don't know. They usually think branding is about pretty logos, colors, and websites. Or, workbooks and presentations, as in the case of Daniel.

I curtly responded, "We don't just design presentations and workbooks. We help people create and manage their brands. In your mind, are you clear on your brand?"

His answer was no.

Fast forward a couple of months, and Daniel decided to go through the branding process. He drove to New York City and within minutes, I had to address his company name.

As usual, I started with a question, "Why is your company called EarthStar18? To be frank, it reminds me of Battlestar Galactica or a similar sci-fi movie. Is this what you want?"

Daniel continued to defend the name. "We chose Earth-

Star18 for several very important and meaningful reasons," he said. "It's important that I share the entire story with you."

"'Earth' is the reason we exist here," he shared. "We each have a unique purpose, but as one we all share in a core foundational purpose, and that is to serve the earth. We are meant to serve the earth as being vessels allowing the light from above to flow through us. As we do this, our physical human bodies anchor the light from above into the earth to help with her ascension. The earth is needed on a larger scale in the universe to bring balance in that light and dark, so she is ascending to a higher vibration to bring the light into balance in the universe at this time, and as humans, we are all participating in this shift and ascension process."

He went on, "The word 'Star' is about us as humans, meaning all humanity. We are reflections of the light from the stars above in the universe, sharing life with this planet. We all have a star in our hearts, and when we return to a place of wholeness and completeness and remember that all we are is love and we follow our heart, the star lights up in our hearts. We are all here to shine our light on Earth; hence, we are all Earthstars."

"The number '18' has significance in many ways," he said. "In numerology, if you add the one and eight together you get nine—the number of 'completion.' We know that our work here is already complete as we chose this mission before arrival and that our lives are truly about remembering all the steps along the way that have already happened to complete our mission and fulfill our destiny."

"My birthday is June eighteenth which, in the secret language of birthdays, represents the 'Day of Financial Security.' Along with that, there is a series called the Fibonacci sequence which details the natural order of how all of life in nature grows on the planet. The Fibonacci sequence is about infinite numbers, and the golden ratio is always divided into 6.18, which is also my birth date and energetically means 'has the power to give life.'"

He went on to tell me even more about the power of the number eighteen and how integral it was to his business and his mission in the world. He had clearly thought about his company name and how it related to the work he did.

After learning about the depth and power of the name, I explained to Daniel, "If you want to make your work more accessible to the masses, you need to use plain English language. Even in your company name. While I understand the significance, 'EarthStar18' is too abstract. More importantly, no one will remember the name. You should change EarthStar18 to simply 'Infinite Beginnings.' Same story. Same message. But, a more evocative and memorable name."

He was blown away by how the new name was simple yet just as powerful.

On a side note: a year later, after properly going through the complete rebranding process, we finally fulfilled on redesigning his workbooks and presentations. They now are more authentic and an accurate representation of his brand.

"The branding process was so transformational," says Daniel Hyman of Infinite Beginnings. "Our new name is professional and has a purpose behind it. It is relevant and practical. My brand makes it easier for me to reflect exactly what I do and how I present."

IS YOUR NAME HARD TO PRONOUNCE OR HARD TO REMEMBER?

Gretchen Cawthon and Trina Fisher combined their talents to open a digital marketing agency—called Thyme Design—which focused on wellness influencers. They knew that they needed a rebrand because their brand and company name were holding them back. Their potential clients didn't connect with their services as well as Gretchen and Trina would have liked.

They went through our brand strategy and naming process, and one of the things we uncovered was their unique fusion of a right brain/left brain approach to their services. Going through a naming process, we arrived at a new name, "Left Right Labs." This new name and brand enabled us to transform their messaging to cater to their ideal target audiences.

"Our previous company name pigeonholed us as just another design firm when our real superpower was our strategy," says Gretchen. "The evolution of our brand and subsequent name change to Left Right Labs has opened opportunities for us to connect with the right audience and work with bigger clients." Her partner Trina says, "The new company name identifies what makes our approach to brand strategy different from other agencies, and our clients completely understand the meaning."

ACTION STEPS FOR AN AUTHENTIC NAME

1. Decide if your name is authentic to your brand—or not. If it's authentic, congratulations, move on to chapter five.
2. If your brand's name is not authentic and you want to explore other options, determine what *type* of name you want: Real World or Coined.
3. Real World Name examples include:
    A. Literal (e.g., American Airlines, Bed Bath and Beyond, The Container Store)
    B. Figurative (e.g., Amazon.com)
    C. Personal/Personal Initials (e.g., Tom Ford, Jimmy Choo, DKNY)

D. Acronym (e.g., 3G, EY, NBC)

E. Misspelled (e.g., Tumblr, Etsy, Xoom, Reddit)

F. Foreign (e.g., Hyundai, Lufthansa)

4. Coined Name examples include:

   A. Compound (e.g., Facebook, YouTube, Birchbox, FitBit)

   B. Suggestive (e.g., Frigidaire, Kleenex)

   C. Artificial (e.g., Altria, Kodak)

   D. Alternate spellings (e.g., Clinique, Google)

5. Develop a list of three to five "Naming Criteria" for evaluating your name options. Do this before you begin brainstorming. The following are examples of naming criteria:

   A. Is it easy to remember?

   B. Is it easy to pronounce?

   C. Does it work across different languages?

   D. Are there any negative connotations?

   E. Is the URL available for purchase?

   F. Could the name be confused with anything else?

   G. Does the name help tell our brand story?

   H. Is the name trademark-able?

   I. Will the name work well with or help endorse the other products, services, or offerings of the business?

   J. Does the name have gravitas or emotional appeal?

   K. Will the name appeal to your target audiences?

6. Have fun as you brainstorm all your naming options. Anything is fair game in this step.

7. With every name, there will always be "pros" and "cons." Evaluate each name according to your chosen criteria. Essentially, the naming criteria will help determine the winner. However, if you're still undecided and have two or three options that remain viable, simply map out a pros and cons list and make a decision based on which name you're willing to accept both the pros and cons.

If you need inspiration to help you brainstorm names, please download *The Naming Guide: 7 Steps to a New Name* e-book online at https://brandingforthepeople.com/resources.

CHAPTER FIVE

An Inauthentic Purpose

WHAT IS YOUR WHY?

Simon Sinek, the author of the book *Start with Why*,[7] says that "People don't buy what you do; they buy *why* you do it." He goes on to say that the companies who inspire people, as opposed to manipulating them, are the ones who perpetually achieve remarkable business success.

My brand theory is consistent with this philosophy. I think a brand should have a clear WHY—a Brand Purpose—so that it not only attracts but inspires and engages loyal fans and raving customers.

Consider the following Brand Purpose examples from these big companies:

---

[7] Simon Sinek, Start with Why: How Great Leaders Inspire Everyone to Take Action (New York: Portfolio, 2009) 41.

Amazon	To offer our customers the lowest possible prices, the best available selection, and the utmost convenience.
Patagonia	To build the best product, cause no unnecessary harm, and use business to inspire and implement solutions to the environmental crisis.

Also, consider the following Brand Purpose statements from some of our small business clients:

Changing Habits	To influence how our food is produced, classified, and marketed.
Syntratech	To bring a radical, non-pharma approach to normalizing blood glucose for people with diabetes.
Amazing	To make amazing lives possible by helping entrepreneurial people build their brands on Amazon.
The Mimic Method	To be the first truly effective language learning program that helps people break through cultural barriers.
Purple Care	To create stronger, harder-working, friendlier, and more beautiful communities, from the ground up.
Thorben	To turn IT headaches into profit-growth systems for organizations who are working to make the world more extraordinary.

When launching a new business, product, or service, your Brand Purpose can be the single most compelling differentiator and tool to create awareness and attract your target audiences. Your target audiences need to know who you are, what you're offering, and how they can benefit. If they don't know who you are, how can you possibly get them to buy your products or services? And, once they know who you are, you have a small window to capture their interest ¬d gain their trust.

For service-based businesses, this is particularly important because people buy from other people they trust, admire, and respect. And when your Brand Purpose is clear, you come across as confident. And confidence builds trust.

Some experts argue that the path to brand awareness and trust is direct marketing and sales. And, this is where a business that leads with marketing differs from one that leads with branding. While marketing gets you in front of your target audiences, branding confirms the clarity and accuracy of your desired message and perception *before* getting in front of them. Your Brand Purpose ensures people are aware of you for the right reasons.

Because you have a small window of time to appeal to your target audiences, do your homework and clarify your Brand Purpose. Don't invest valuable time or money marketing to them, only to lose their interest forever because your Brand Purpose was ambiguous, and they didn't resonate with it.

Once you've defined your Brand Purpose, the next step is to determine the best marketing channels and vehicles through which to share it. In order to determine your ideal channels:

1. Find out where your target audiences live, work, and play. Figure out what they read and what they listen to, plus who they follow or what events they attend. The

goal is to understand their psychographic profile, so you know how best to connect with them.

2. Determine which communication platforms your company is most comfortable with (or willing to invest in). For some businesses, online marketing is the primary vehicle, whether it's advertising on Facebook, Instagram, LinkedIn, YouTube, or Pinterest. For other businesses, print or magazine ads, billboards, or outdoor signage are the favored channels. And yet for others, the affiliate model (partnering with other businesses for recognition) is the preferred vehicle. Still others might prefer events.

When I started my branding company in 2010, I chose a relatively non-traditional approach to creating brand awareness. Since I didn't have the technical know-how for online marketing and had zero advertising budget, I created my own platform by hosting an event. This felt like a natural and authentic way for me to share my Brand Purpose.

It wasn't easy, but it was worth it. I filled the room with fifty-six attendees, and because I shared my Brand Purpose and created value for each attendee, I generated my first six-figures in revenue—a humbling and impressive accomplishment for someone who had just started a company with no list, no marketing budget, and not even a book such as this one. I simply had a Brand Purpose and a message to share. That message put me on the map. The event's success snowballed my brand awareness, leading to other lucrative opportunities.

When a startup tells me that they don't need a brand right away, I share my personal story to inspire them and show that your brand can ultimately lead you on a successful journey. You may not need all the tools in the branding toolkit, but if you start with a Brand Purpose, you'll be light years ahead of other business owners.

IS YOUR PURPOSE MEMORABLE?

Afrin Khan came to me because she had a dream to start her own event planning company. She has a passion for elephants, and she loves the color red. Her company name naturally became Red Elephant Events. Not only was she thrilled to start her company, but her friends were excited for her as well. One particularly generous friend offered to create her logo. Afrin had heard me preach that branding was so much more than a logo, but she still enthusiastically came to ask, "What do you think of the logo for my new company?"

RED ELEPHANT EVENTS

I took one look at it, and lovingly said, "Well, for starters, it's quite *literal*, don't you think? It's one big, red, elephant!"

Somewhat deflated, she admitted that she agreed. We both laughed.

But she was curious about what else I thought. I continued, "It looks like clip art, and it's kind of cheesy-looking—and I don't see you as a cheesy person." A generic clip art image might not register consciously with her target audience, but they will know that the logo feels unprofessional.

"In addition, this clip art mock-up is inauthentic to who you are, because this is an *African* elephant and you're from Bangladesh, a South Asian country. I understand you love elephants, but this is the *wrong* elephant for your brand. Surely, we can do better than this, right?"

Afrin and I worked together for several months to uncover the deeper meaning of her brand. We started by creating her Brand Purpose. Through a series of discussions, we landed on the idea: A Future of Memorable Experiences.

This Brand Purpose became the inspiration for her brand and her Visual Identity. Rather than using the African elephant, we decided to use a less obvious representation of an elephant (without an easy reference to African or Asian culture). From a storytelling perspective, we emphasized the forward movement of the elephant. Science has proven that elephants have incredible memories, so we used that factual component and infused it into her Brand Purpose. Elephants transport memories...into the future.

We chose a particular red for the elephant because the color symbolizes strength and power. However, we introduced a couple of other unexpected colors, which included ivory (a nod to elephant tusks) and turquoise (which coincidentally was a prominent color at Afrin's Indian wedding).

Afrin was amazed at the use of a Brand Purpose to inspire her brand and inspire a stunning Visual Identity. As a result,

Red Elephant created an immediate stampede in the marketplace and a herd of raving fans. Not only did she easily launch her business, but she effortlessly attracted clients. In the first five months, she generated twenty-seven proposals and planned seventeen events. A year later, with so much business, her husband, Iman, quit his job and joined forces as her business partner. Today, they run a seven-figure event planning and speaker training company and continue to use the Visual Identity initially created as a result of her clear Brand Purpose.

IS YOUR PURPOSE MORE THAN JUST MAKING MONEY?

Nick Unsworth, a young entrepreneurial marketer, found himself depressed and aimless after achieving what should have been a significant milestone and highlight of his life—selling his business by the age of thirty. The realization that selling a business wasn't the end-all be-all led him on a quest to build a new business that had a deep and meaningful purpose, other than just making money.

His then-business coach, Suzanne Evans suggested the company name "Life on Fire." Immediately, he fell in love with this new name. In three words, it described everything he wanted in a business. A business that would enable people to live energetic and exhilarating lives. He wanted his brand to be equally as exciting. He wanted his branding to be perfect right out of the gate, and so we decided to work together.

During the branding process, Nick admitted that selling his business had left him unfulfilled. He shared that he really wanted to create a business that was meaningful and fulfilling. He wanted to ensure that his life and those of his clients weren't just about work and money. He believed that life should focus on family, friends, and relationships.

During one of our sessions, he admitted that he was currently focused on a product launch, and he was bummed that he couldn't attend his best friend's bachelor party and wedding. He had recently moved to San Diego, and his best friend lived on the East Coast. He felt that traveling would take too much time out of his already busy schedule.

After listening to his story, I asked him, "Would not attending your best friend's bachelor party AND wedding, because of a product launch be out of integrity or inauthentic with living a 'life on fire?'"

In that moment, he realized the truth. How could he possibly own Life on Fire when he wasn't embodying it himself? This realization inspired me to crystallize his Brand Purpose into the following storyline:

There are three questions entrepreneurs ask themselves:

- What am I **worth**?
- What is my business **worth**?
- What is my life **worth**?

The answers are:

- **Worth** comes from within (having a positive mindset)
- **Worth** defines what you do (a business you love)
- **Worth** creates a community (people who need you)

However, it's not the destination; it's the **journey**. But the **journey** is **worth** it only if you're an entrepreneur who makes money and makes a difference with and for other people.

The final result—his Brand Purpose is articulated in four words: **A Journey Worth Living.**

I showed him this idea in a creative mock-up to help him see that this Brand Purpose was already a part of him.

"The business completely took off with the new brand," Nick said. "It was contagious, like wildfire. Five years later, I'm still living the brand that was created. I've never been more in alignment. We continue to attract our ideal clients, and we're poised to be more profitable than we've ever been. I live my brand every single day, and it guides my decisions because I ask myself regularly, "Am I living my Brand Purpose and a life on fire?" and "How can I help others live their lives on fire?"

IS YOUR PURPOSE A BUSINESS MODEL?

After helping Nick Unsworth with his brand, he recommended me to Cole Hatter, who was the top speaker for multimillionaire Than Merrill's Fortune Builders, a premier real estate education company. While already successful, Cole too was on a quest, similar to Nick's, to create a brand that was truly and authentically aligned with his life's purpose—and that purpose was more than just to make money.

After an eleven-hour Brand Strategy day with Cole Hatter at his home in Costa Mesa, I helped him visualize his Brand Purpose in a framework. We called it the "4 Quadrants." Essentially, here is the concept:

There are two axes. The X-axis is about having a purpose in life. The Y-axis about money or "profit." When you populate each box within the quadrant with actions and aspects of your life, the resulting image tells a story. For Cole, it shows that he has lived his life authentically. He believes that thriving is the same as living your life authentically. When you enter your own personal information, you can see how to approach your life authentically as well.

In the bottom left quadrant, you'll find entrepreneurs who have little to no purpose and also aren't making money or profit. These people are in the "Suffering" quadrant.

In the bottom right quadrant, are people and companies who are extremely purposeful, e.g., missionaries, nonprofit organizations, but have limited funds or profits. These people are in the "Giving" quadrant.

In the upper left quadrant are entrepreneurs and business owners who are making a lot of money and profit but are aimless and lack purpose in life. We decided to call this quadrant "Earning."

Lastly, the upper right quadrant represents Cole's purpose—this quadrant is called "Thriving." This quadrant is about having a deep and meaningful purpose AND making a profit. With both, you're able to have a much more significant impact. You're able to "Thrive and Make Money Matter."

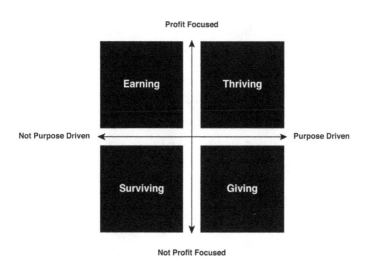

These four quadrants became the basis for his signature conference called "Thrive: Make Money Matter." Today, it is a highly successful, annual three-day conference. Within a short time, he built a tribe of like-minded entrepreneurs and has attracted the likes of Robert Herjavec, Gary Vaynerchuk, Jack Canfield, JJ Virgin, Tai Lopez, and Dave Asprey (to name a few big names) who convene at his conference to inspire and teach other entrepreneurs to build a "for purpose" business that goes beyond just making money, but focuses on making money matter to create a positive impact and a legacy.

ACTION STEPS FOR AN AUTHENTIC PURPOSE

1. Do you have a Brand Purpose?
   A. If yes, perfect. But, check in to see if it's still alive and inspiring to you right now. If it is, great! If not, or if your Brand Purpose does not motivate you into action each day, it might be time to revisit your Brand Purpose (go to Step 2).
2. Brainstorm (on a whiteboard, a journal, or a clean sheet of paper) the answers to the following questions:
   A. Besides making money, why are you in this business?
   B. What problems do you want to solve? And, for whom?
   C. Why do you want to help these people? Why do you care about them?
   D. Would you be in business if you knew you were going to fail at it?
   E. If money wasn't an object, what business would you create?
   F. Is there a problem in your community or in the world that you want to solve?
   G. Why should people buy your product or service over other products or services?
3. Keep brainstorming until you have a palette of words

and sentences to draw upon and find the singular most compelling reason (your purpose) for your brand.

4. Take your most compelling "why" and use it to write your Brand Purpose in the form of a statement. See the examples in this chapter for sentence structure. Here are my tips and criteria for writing a powerful Brand Purpose:

   A. Describes "why the brand exists."
   B. Uses twenty-one words or less.
   C. Includes target audience, industry/category, or core offerings.
   D. Is aspirational or evokes an emotion.
   E. Is written in the personality, tone, and voice of your brand.

Advanced: If you're a creative writer, one popular way to express your Brand Purpose is through a Brand Story or a Manifesto. The Brand Story or Manifesto communicates who your company is and what it does in terms that are relevant and meaningful to your target audiences. It is not just a glorified mission statement. Rather than just communicating the facts, it is charged with emotion and conveys passion and purpose. The Brand Story can be a PDF that's shared with clients, or it can be turned into a compelling video.

CHAPTER SIX

An Inauthentic Message

A CONFUSED MIND SAYS NO

There's a common saying among branding and marketing professionals: "A confused mind always says no." This philosophy has driven me to explain branding in a way that is clear and easy to understand. I want more people to understand branding so they can take action with it. My goal with branding is to help people get crystal clear on who they are, how they will go to market, and what they will say in their communications. With this clarity, the probability of a prospect converting to a client dramatically increases.

A company with market confusion or lack of clarity is not internally clear about what they do. If you're not clear on what you do, ask yourself, "how does my company make money?" I also ask companies to tell me what they offer customers. Are you going to coach them? Are you going to help them do something, or are you going to sell them a product, a program, a service, or a subscription?

If a company has a conversion problem, often it's because they are not clearly explaining the benefits of their products or services. If you fall into this camp, a potential customer might ask, "I understand that you offer six months of coaching, but what are these six months going to do for me?" This company's brand hasn't already coherently answered this question.

A confusing message can either attract the wrong people to your business or hinder sales conversions. It may even impact the company's ability to communicate the full depth and breadth of its offerings. Consider the following examples of our clients who had inauthentic messages that created market confusion.

IS YOUR MESSAGE RELEVANT TO YOUR TARGET AUDIENCES?

Laura Spaulding of Spaulding Decon had built a successful business in the crime scene, meth lab, and hoarding cleanup industry. Based in Florida, she had a goal to grow the business into a national franchise brand. I did not have a portfolio of clientele in this industry, but I knew that the branding process works no matter the industry. And I was up for the challenge.

I started the process by auditing her current branding and messaging. Upon visiting her website, the first message "above the fold" said, "When tragedy strikes, Spaulding Decon is there." The images throughout the website were downright frightening—crime and homicide scenes, blood and guts. Really gory stuff that most people couldn't stomach. Even worse, Laura posted these same images on social media. To top things off, her website was covered in a primary red color. I didn't need to ask her why red. It was apparent that this color represents her line of work. It turns out that the imagery, colors, and messaging on the site attracted a lot of attention.

My first comment to Laura was, "Why are you showing all of these gory images? No one wants to see that."

She responded, "Yes, they do. People have voyeuristic behaviors. We get many hits on our site late at night from people viewing these images."

My next question was an important one, and it would be the very question that would completely shift Laura's mindset about her branding and messaging. I asked, "That's great that you're getting all this traffic, but do these people pay you for your services?"

Her answer was a flat, "No."

There were two problems that Spaulding Decon needed to address to make their brand message more authentic to their brand. They needed to identify the right target audience (who would pay for their services), and they needed to craft a message that was relevant to *them*. They had the wrong message and they were going after the wrong target audience—one that didn't even pay for their services.

The solution to both problems was to simply follow the money. Who do you think pays for these services? Most people would say it's the families or the police department. It's not. If you guessed insurance companies and apartment complex owners, you're spot on. Laura had an aha moment! Spaulding Decon had created a B2C (business-to-consumer) brand message when they really needed to build a B2B (business-to-business) brand message.

The key takeaway here is to take an outside-in approach and first understand your target audiences before crafting your message. So, that's exactly what we did. Through an in-depth brand exploration exercise, we narrowed down a stronger, more relevant message that would resonate with potential buyers—insurance companies and apartment complex owners.

The message "When tragedy strikes, Spaulding Decon is there" makes the target audience think of Spaulding Decon *after* the tragedy. Instead, I recommended that they transform their message to the context of having them think of Spaulding Decon long *before* tragedy strikes.

Sound familiar? That's the way people think about insurance companies.

I recommended changing the brand message to "Restoring Peace of Mind," assuring their target audiences that Spaulding Decon would be there to come in and clean up the mess *if and when* a tragedy struck.

The brand message was now authentic because it was relevant. It was the right message for the right audience. After the shift in messaging, Laura reported, "I was surprised by the detailed dissection required to define a brand, logo, and message. I wish I had taken the step ten years ago. Changing the brand was hard, but I feel like it was the best decision for the future of my company."

After the rebrand, Spaulding Decon succeeded in its goal of converting to a franchise model. Formerly only in Florida, the company now also operates in California, Georgia, Ohio, Michigan, North Carolina, South Carolina, Pennsylvania, and Texas.

IS YOUR MESSAGE ATTRACTING THE WRONG PEOPLE?

When I first started my company, I joined a business "mastermind"—which is essentially a curated group of other like-minded business owners. In one of the offsite meetings, each member was tasked with doing a presentation that included making a pitch to sell something.

I loved putting together stories through presentations, so this was right up my alley. When it was my turn, I gave my presentation as usual but making an offer after teaching was new for me. I did it anyway.

When I finished, the mastermind leader, Suzanne Evans, exclaimed, "Oh my God! We have to hire you!" She said she had never thought of branding in the same way I had presented it. She thought branding was just logos, colors, and websites. She never considered that branding was about how people perceive you, and what people say about you after you leave the room. Needless to say, I was thrilled to have the privilege of branding the mastermind leader.

Like many companies I've worked with, Suzanne already had a successful business. While she was a brilliant leader, marketer, and speaker, she was experiencing brand shame. She was hesitant to share her brand with potential clients because it did not represent her—she had a rudimentary "mom and pop" brand.

I met with Suzanne and Melonie Orr (her life and business partner) for a Brand Strategy day. I started my line of questioning with, "What is the *one* problem that you want to solve through rebranding?"

I was looking for an answer beyond, "Our current logo is terrible, and we're ashamed of it." They were on the same page with their responses, "Our brand message says, 'Help More People,' and we think it's attracting the wrong type of clients. It's attracting people who think of themselves as 'broken' and looking for Suzanne Evans to act as their savior."

Suzanne is not the "soft, nurturing type" business coach. Rather, she's the "tell-it-like-it-is" and "in-your-face" business coach with a strong personality. So, I argued that her brand message of "Help More People" was completely inauthentic and did not position her brand effectively. It was no wonder she was attracting the wrong people. Ironically these people were willing to hand over money, but she didn't want it because they weren't the right fit for her coaching. They weren't ready to take her advice and move themselves to the next level.

To help Suzanne attract the ideal audience, I came up with a new message for her brand. It was three words: "The Other Side." This wasn't a tagline. Instead, it was the underlying message that drove all other messages. "The Other Side" was the basis to tell the story about how Suzanne helps her clients go from broke to making money. From stuck to unstuck. From indecisive to decisive. From corporate to entrepreneurship. And, since we wanted to leverage her strong personality, we also felt it was appropriate to rebrand the company to just her name—Suzanne Evans (similar to many other leading coaches in her space who are known as their Personal Brand).

Suzanne is now a *New York Times* best-selling author, she hit the Inc. 500/5000 five years in a row and grew her business to seven million dollars in revenue with fifteen full-time employees in just five years. After rebranding, Suzanne reported, "Before rebranding, I had brand shame. My business had hit the million-dollar mark, and we were really fortunate to have great digital marketing to do well in business. However, our branding was holding us back. After the rebrand, everything changed. We started to attract our ideal clients and repel the ones we didn't want to work with. Our revenues tripled. Our web traffic increased by 4,000 percent. We made the Inc. 500 list three years in a row and grew our business with new verticals."

IS YOUR MESSAGE DISRUPTIVE?

Williamsburg Learning is a remarkable online high school with impressive programs. They were doing well financially, but they didn't want to rest on their laurels. The president and co-founder, James Ure, had a vision to reframe the conversation around alternative education, and he wanted a brand to differentiate his company in this budding industry. Their current brand message didn't represent their product nor speak to the audience they wanted to reach, and their visuals, which used an old colonial-style font, made them seem old, stodgy, and outdated. It certainly wasn't authentic to their educational philosophy, i.e., innovative, fresh, and revolutionary. Their core philosophy of teaching students *how* to think, not *what* to think, needed to be known to more parents—and their brand needed to establish instant credibility with parents who would entrust them with the education of their children. They wanted a brand message that was not only disruptive but compelling and inspiring.

When they decided to develop a new program, they thought the timing was perfect to revisit their brand message and finally go through the branding process. Similar to other branding projects, the starting point was to deepen the understanding of their target audiences and craft a brand message that appealed to them. Through a series of strategy sessions, we synthesized their new brand message: Liberate the Magic.

"Liberate the Magic" was a new and revolutionary brand message beyond anything they'd communicated before. Everything started to fall in place once we defined that message, because it hit all the criteria they were looking for in a new brand message. Furthermore, it not only reinvigorated the entire organization around a singular message; it gave my design team the necessary inspiration for Williamsburg Learning's new Visual Identity. Compared to their old Visual Identity, which used dull, boring colors, their new Visual Identity used primary colors, subconsciously reminding us of school with the infusion of a magical component.

Shortly after launching the new brand and message, James Ure said, "As an alternative high school, it is critical that our brand message appeals to both parents and children.

That's no easy task. Our new brand message helped Williamsburg Learning stand out, but when we announced our new online program, we beat our stretch goal of filling it in eight weeks. Instead, we filled it in a record two weeks!"

That's the power of a disruptive and authentic brand message!

ACTION STEPS FOR AN AUTHENTIC MESSAGE

1. Write down ALL of the problems that you solve for your target audiences and organize them in the following three categories (see more in chapter ten):
   A. Functional problems
   B. Economic problems
   C. Emotional problems
2. Once you have all of the problems listed, turn each into a statement that solves the problem.
3. The next step is to evaluate each statement/message and determine if there's ONE that supersedes all the others and could serve as the umbrella message. Use the following criteria to evaluate each one:
   A. Is the message relevant to all of our target audiences?
   B. Is the solution unique or different in the competitive landscape?
   C. Is the message something you can credibly deliver on?

4. Choose the message that delivers best on all three criteria.

5. Optional: If you're not able to shortlist the message to only one, another approach is to shortlist the top three messages and test these messages with your target audiences to see which one resonates the most.

CHAPTER SEVEN

An Inauthentic Personality

PROFESSIONAL IS NOT A PERSONALITY

The Greek philosopher Aristotle taught that a solid argument or belief is based on three pillars: Ethos (Credibility), Logos (Logic), and Pathos (Emotion). Similarly, we first buy based on emotion, and then we validate our emotional buy with logic and reason. Just as with a solid argument, these three pillars are involved in the sales process.

Rather than competing on cost, you want to compete on value. In order to compete on value, you need to appeal to all three pillars: credibility, logic, and emotion. Further, I recommend that you take it up a notch and compete on personality. Competing on personality is far more compelling than competing on cost or even value as a whole, because when a buyer makes a purchasing decision, they're making it based on their emotional connection and alignment with the brand's personality. Even Target and Walmart, while they are positioned as "low cost," each brand embodies different personalities. If you want to continue competing on price, you'll quickly find that there will always be someone who will undercut you or someone who can deliver a service for less.

Other companies will compete with you in different ways. Some of the competition variables are within your control, and some are not. For example, you can't control purchasing decisions if they're based on physical proximity. If a client wants to hire a company that is located in the same city or country as they are, but you don't have a physical presence there, your brand personality won't be able to help. If the CEO of a client has a college friend or relative working at a particular company, then he/she has preferential status over you and your brand personality will have a hard time competing.

In general, if you find that your target audiences see the value in your products or services AND can afford them, but you're still competing on price, your company has a branding problem—unless you're Walmart, in which case, "lowest price" is a key part of your brand proposition.

When it comes to branding, you *can* control your brand personality. *Every* brand should clarify its personality. Some brands are funny. Some are charismatic. Some are nurturing. Some are obnoxious. Some are rebellious. Personality attributes are a key part of expressing a brand. They make your marketing efforts stronger by helping you connect better with your target audience. More importantly, every company must own their brand personality, and never stray from it.

But there's one pitfall to avoid.

Never create your brand personality around being "professional." Why? Because *professional* is not a personality. If you have the credentials, experience, and expertise and you get paid for it, then you are a professional. Professional doesn't mean anything more than that, and it doesn't set you apart from your competitors. Customers will expect that you're a professional, but they will likely buy (or not buy) because of your personality.

I like to illustrate the distinction between professional and personality by showing pictures of the following talk show hosts.

- Rosie O'Donnell
- Ellen DeGeneres
- Oprah
- Wendy Williams
- Dr. Phil

Each of these celebrities is a professional. But each of them built their brand (and careers) on their distinct personalities. Their brand personality helps them become recognized for what they are known for. Their brand personality gives us an indicator of what we expect of them in the future.

We watch Ellen DeGeneres because we want to laugh and feel good. We turn to Dr. Phil for some tough love and psychiatry. You can love them or hate them, but they have each carved out a niche for themselves by owning it and amplifying their brand personality. And, sticking to their brand personality keeps them authentic. It would be disturbingly inauthentic if Rosie O'Donnell were to suddenly be nurturing. Or if Oprah started shouting at her audience, cursing with the same brashness as the entrepreneur and marketing powerhouse Gary Vaynerchuk.

If you are completely honest, what is your company's brand personality? Or, when people describe your company, what do they say? Is your company considered funny? Warm? Direct? Is there a disconnect between how you want your brand personality to be perceived and what others *think* is your personality? Be yourself and allow your brand to be what it is without pretense. People connect with authenticity, and when you're authentic, it shouldn't take extra work.

Your brand personality is the best way to not only differentiate yourself but to connect with your target audiences on an emotional level. Your ideal clients and customers want to know who you are and what you care about. Share your history, both good and bad, to help your customers connect with you on a deeper level than they would if you just shared the logical and reasoning side of your company (although you'll want to appeal to those factors as well). Just be you! People will appreciate your personality, and ultimately do business with you because they're clear on who you are. They know what they're signing up for. Don't use your brand personality as a gimmick to simply grab attention. Rather, use it to weed out those who are not your target audiences.

That said, there are a few things to keep in mind after you define your brand personality and begin expressing it in your marketing campaigns.

IS YOUR PERSONALITY A COLOR?

One of the tools used to express a brand personality is the use of color, particularly when the color is an unexpected, unpredictable, and easily identifiable color in the competitive landscape.

Consider the following examples of mobile phone companies that use color to differentiate themselves:

T-Mobile = Pink

Verizon = Red and black
AT&T = Blue
Sprint = Yellow

Following this line of thinking, we were challenged to rebrand a Fort Worth-based company called Xtreme Lawn Care. The CEO, Justin Berg, approached our firm because he felt they had outgrown their name and brand. The company expanded into different businesses, and he felt the term "Lawn Care" in their name had become limiting. It didn't describe the full depth and breadth of their services: lawn care, landscaping, pest control, and tree services for both residential and commercial properties in the greater Fort Worth area. Even if they wanted to keep the name, Justin didn't like the idea of Xtreme Lawn, Xtreme Trees, Xtreme Pest Control. Furthermore, lawn care was the most labor-intensive service offering (with the lowest profitability margins), and they didn't want to continue highlighting only this service.

Make your neighbors green with envy.

According to Justin, "We knew we were losing business. We would arrive at a customer's house and notice a tree company had already been there. We would ask the customer why they didn't hire us. The customer usually responded, 'We didn't know you did trees.'" Justin was tired of losing business from his long-standing customers.

He was also adamant that the new brand maintains the use of the color purple because people recognize them as the "purple people." Of course, we agreed to honor this request. We even pushed it further by recommending that they double down and own the color purple as part of their new brand name and change from Xtreme Lawn Care to Purple Care. The rationale was that "Purple" was a color they wanted to own, and "Care" was a more customer-centric, friendly term that had the right personality, as opposed to the personality conveyed with "Xtreme."

After persuading Justin and his team that this was the right name for the future trajectory of their business (because they weren't thrilled with it at first), they finally agreed to move forward.

Justin recalls, "At the time, I realized I was in the old mind-set. Eventually, I embraced Purple Care because it broke me free from my old way of thinking. It forced me to change. And, we all know that people hate change—sometimes people fight change, literally to their death. But, since I believe the only thing constant in life is change, I agreed to be open-minded and accept the name change."

It was a massive change for Justin, but he saw a bright future ahead with his brand name signaling a company with a unique brand personality in the industry.

"You know what the new name Purple Care did for me?" Justin reported. "It got people to ask me the golden question: What exactly is Purple Care?" That question gave him the opportunity to tell their story. Justin continues to report that his response is always, "We're a full-service lawn care, landscape, tree service, and pest control company. We have experts in every department. We have sharpshooters in every division."

Justin explains that clients are now calling them even for things they don't do. He's happy that they're calling. According to Justin, "My branding is working. They see purple, and they assume it's us. I love it. The reason we have 'Care' in the name is that we care more than our competitors. We care about the quality of work. We care about what we do."

Just months after the rebrand, a long-standing customer came to Justin and asked, "Why Purple Care?" After Justin explained the story behind the new brand, the very next question the customer asked was, "You guys do fences? I didn't know that!"

He told him, "I changed the name so that YOU can ask that question."

Justin walked out of his customer's home with a $7,000 sale. And, as he was leaving, his customer yelled, "Hey Justin, I guess that new brand worked, didn't it?"

"Yes, it did!" said Justin, celebrating.

IS YOUR PERSONALITY CONSISTENT ONLINE AND OFFLINE?

Malorie Tadimi looked like a Republican housewife.

Well, her online photos did.

In reality, Malorie was a playful entrepreneur working in the management consultant space. With an impressive background, having worked with Fortune 500 companies and high-performing tech ventures, her online brand personality wasn't consistent with her offline, in-person brand personality. Her branding looked homemade, but her in-personality was sophisticated and high-end, yet personable and down-to-earth. Her branding needed to convey all of these personality characteristics.

Malorie knew there was a fine line between having a brand personality that's aspirational and authentic. She wanted a brand that was genuine and one that she would be proud of. She wasn't just another business consultant or coach.

Here's the deal. You can be aspirational with your branding but be sure not to present yourself as someone you are not. I've seen people buy an Armani suit and rent a mansion or Lamborghini for a photoshoot in order to present themselves as uber-successful (think Wolf of Wall Street and Jordan Belfort posing on a yacht). There is nothing wrong with presenting a high-end, aspirational image, but it is inauthentic if you are struggling financially and just getting your business off the ground.

Malorie let us tackle a full brand overhaul. As we do with all of our branding engagements, we needed to clarify her brand purpose, her brand message, and her brand personality, prior to tackling her Visual Identity. We also encouraged her to hire a photographer and stylist to match the rest of her branding.

The results were stunning.

Her new branding, visuals, and photography were bold and confident—and unique compared to the other coaches and consultants who've been in business for years. Malorie's brand resonates with the specific people that she wants to attract.

MALORIE

"Building my brand created the confidence and consistency I was missing in my business," says Malorie. "It now ensures that I present myself and my company in the most authentic way. My brand resonates with my target audiences because it's both aspirational and approachable. Consequently, my website converts at a much higher rate. It's a complete one-eighty." With over five hundred thousand followers on Facebook after just one year with her new brand, she fast-tracked her business to seven figures (and is still growing)—a goal many aspiring and established coaches and consultants only aspire to achieve.

IS YOUR PERSONALITY STUCK IN THE '90s?

Dr. Al Spicer is a well-trained premium executive coach for high-performing Fortune 500 executives. However, his branding looked dated, as if he hadn't touched it since the early '90s. It didn't reflect a high-end premium feel that would command a premium price for his services. He came across as a bootstrapped, mass-market amateur brand. As such, he needed to update his brand personality to accurately reflect where he is today.

Additionally, in going through the branding process, we felt that his company name, Action for Breakthrough, didn't convey a premium feel. He admitted that he'd been told by a business coach that his company name needed to be descriptive and explain a benefit for his customers. Poor advice? Not exactly. While the thinking was accurate, the higher-order advantage of using his service was far more significant than just taking actions to have a breakthrough. His audiences would be more inspired and driven to hire him as their coach if he articulated the real benefit of retaining his services. That is, to live an extraordinary life. Luckily, we learned that Al had already owned the domain ExtraordinaryLife.com for fifteen years. We couldn't believe it and agreed it was time for the name to resurface.

Our branding goals were threefold. First, we needed to match his online presence with his offline presence by transforming it from a mass-market brand to a high-end premium brand. Second, we needed to start using the more fitting company name, Extraordinary Life, that he already owned. And, third, we needed to establish a Brand Promise that defined a higher-order benefit that his already-successful clients would be excited to achieve.

EXTRAORDINARY LIFE

The Extraordinary Life Brand Promise became: "Harnessing your Hidden Potential." While not a tagline, it serves as a theme for his messaging. We asked ourselves, "If he helps his clients harness their hidden potential, what will they be able to achieve?" The result? A brand-new theme: "Life. Leadership. Legacy." Finally, using his new Brand Promise and theme, we transformed his entire website and marketing collateral to reflect his authentic brand personality.

IS YOUR PERSONALITY NON-DIFFERENTIATING?

Business and Video Marketing Strategist, Maria Andros, was a fantastic business coach, but her followers knew her as the "video marketing queen." To make matters worse, she looked like every other video marketer out there.

Not only did she need to make it clear to her audience that she was a business coach, but she wanted to command premium prices for her exclusive private coaching services. She wished to attract more discerning clients, so she needed high-level aesthetics and top-shelf design. She desperately wanted to differentiate her brand from her peers and competitors. Her brand personality needed to surface as this was the key ingredient to making this happen.

We worked with Maria to transform her brand to one that imbued her brand personality—premium, high-end, and luxury. These characteristics informed a new Visual Identity, which even included the use of a font that's widely displayed in high fashion. Furthermore, she hired a sought-after New York fashion photographer to shoot new photos.

We thought, "If everyone in the marketing and coaching industry looks mass-market, let's have Maria stand out with a brand personality inspired by Chanel, Gucci, and Burberry. This brand shift was a game changer for her because it not only differentiated her from her competitors but (we later found out) generated Maria over half a million in revenue at her first post-rebrand event. Combined with her passion, marketing savvy, and personal image, her new brand elevated her to an aspirational brand. She was able to effortlessly increase pricing and attract a discerning select group of ideal, private clients.

IS YOUR PERSONALITY BORING?

Odyssey LSAT Tutoring & Test Preparation provides highly effective LSAT preparation through individualized, one-on-one LSAT tutoring. Claiming to help students raise their LSAT score twenty points, they were already successfully acquiring leads online, particularly through Yelp reviews.

The founder, Jonathan McCarty, wanted to take the company's success to the next level. He reached out to me requesting a new website. I explained to him what you've learned so far. That is, branding is so much more than a logo or a website. I explained that in order to develop the best possible website, we needed to take a step back and define the brand and create the corresponding look and feel that expressed his company's brand personality.

LSAT test prep is not necessarily the most creative or sexy industry. Arguably, LSAT test prep is a "boring" industry, so owning a brand personality would prove to be a worthwhile strategy, because we knew that his competitors were outright bland, predictable, institutional, and personality-less.

We brought in brand personality to Odyssey Test Prep by adding color, style, imagery, messaging, and exciting visuals. This transformation enabled his company to easily attract young, ambitious students.

If you're still wondering how brand personality can impact your bottom line, check out the results Jonathan reported shortly after launching the new brand.

"Just thought I'd update you on how the new brand is performing since this is the first month, we've had it up and running. It's been by far our best sales month EVER! Sales are up 399 percent from just last month. The best part is that we now have the opportunity to affect more change in more people and help them realize their LSAT potential. I know that I was a bit hesitant about making the investment when we first spoke, but I've already recouped that investment and more within the first month!"

Four months later, Jonathan reported, "May was Odyssey Test Prep's best month up to that point by a MILE, June was on par with May, July was Odyssey's best month up until that point, August was Odyssey's best month up until that point, and now September is on track to be Odyssey's best month *ever*. Needless to say, we're seeing some phenomenal growth over here!"

Case studies like Jonathan's reinforce my philosophy that brand personality is crucial. Don't be boring. Add zest and pizzazz to your branding. Use brand personality to your advantage. If you don't, you'll leave it to chance and make it difficult for people to decide whether or not they should buy your products or services.

ACTION STEPS FOR AN AUTHENTIC BRAND PERSONALITY

1. On a sheet of clean paper, create two columns:
   A. Label the first column, "Desired Brand Personality." Under the title, list the top five personality attributes you would like to be perceived by your target clients or customers.
   B. Label the second column, "Actual Brand Person-

ality." Ask ten people (preferably those who fit the profile of your target clients or customers) to describe your company's top five personality attributes.

2. Compare the list in each column and determine the degree of alignment or the gap between your *desired* Brand Personality and your *actual* Brand Personality. Are you happy with the result? If not, evaluate all the changes you need to make in your branding to convey the desired Brand Personality you would like to have in the marketplace.

3. Then, make sure your Brand Personality is consistent online and offline.

For a unique tool that's often used to infuse personality into a brand, visit https://brandingforthepeople.com/resources to download our "The Brand Archetypes Guide: 20 Personas to Inspire Your Brand."

CHAPTER EIGHT

An Inauthentic Architecture

WHAT GOT YOU HERE, WON'T GET YOU THERE

Marshall Goldsmith coined a universally true phrase when he wrote his book *What Got You Here, Won't Get You There: How Successful People Become Even More Successful.*[8] In this essential guide for global leaders who are at the top of the ladder or on the way there, Goldsmith helps his readers uncover their (sometimes unconscious) annoying habits, which keep them from attaining a higher level of success.

I believe the same expression holds true for branding, especially for businesses that have achieved great success with or without an authentic brand. The brand that got you to where you are right now, won't get you to where you want

---

8   Michael Goldsmith, What Got You Here, Won't Get You There: How Successful Peop!- -
     Even More Successful (New York, NY: Hachette Books, 2007).

to go. This chapter applies primarily to businesses with multiple divisions, multiple revenue streams, or multiple offerings. If your business is solely based on one product offering you won't immediately apply this knowledge to your business, but it will help you better understand branding as a whole. I would also argue that this section will help you set up the architecture of your brand so that your company can grow strategically.

I love the nimbleness of entrepreneurs. "Speed-to-market" is key for entrepreneurs and small to midsize businesses—it's one of the reasons why I decided to focus on working with them instead of Fortune 500 companies. While there are strong advantages to getting to market first and monetizing an idea, many nimble businesses skip the step of building a Brand Architecture.

What exactly is Brand Architecture?

It's a strategic framework that organizes all of your offerings and determines how to brand (or not brand) them from both a verbal and visual perspective.

If you've been able to generate revenue and your architecture seems to be working, you might be wondering why you should create a Brand Architecture now? Truthfully, most businesses create their Brand Architecture *after* they've demonstrated some initial success and steady revenue. In some cases, however, I've helped early-stage businesses define their Brand Architecture on the outset, because it allowed them to stay focused on the end game. In doing so, we saved them time, money, and energy by creating ONE brand that could encompass multiple offerings and revenue streams.

Self-funded businesses often assume that their brand will either grow and change organically, or they fail to imagine what their business will look like once it has grown. They don't believe they need to think about their Brand Architecture.

Until they do.

Oftentimes, when a business grows beyond its default brand and they expand into a new market, their brand doesn't properly work with or support this expansion. If they had considered their Brand Architecture from the beginning, they might have the framework and tools to expand the brand without diluting it or making it fragmented or disjointed.

Whether you're creating a Brand Architecture in your first five years of business or you're creating a Brand Architecture for the next five years, think of it the same way an architect uses a blueprint to build a house. An architect designs a clear foundation and plan for building a house, right? They define the construction specifications such as dimensions, materials, layouts, and installation methods. In addition, the blueprint makes the project more efficient and cost-effective in the long run because the builders are able to construct a house that meets the homeowners' near-term and long-term needs.

For example, let's say you build a home without a blueprint and you failed to mention that you want a bathroom installed in a particular location, and that location is nowhere near the pre-installed plumbing. What happens after the home is built? One of two things might happen: either you can't install the bathroom in the desired location; or, it may end up costing you a lot more money down the road to establish new plumbing in the desired bathroom location.

Your Brand Architecture works in the same way as a blueprint. With this blueprint, your business builds an ecosystem of brands, in which the value and equity you're creating from one brand can directly and indirectly lend value and equity to the other brands that coexist in the architecture.

There are four broad frameworks to use as models for your Brand Architecture:

Monolithic. In Monolithic Brand Architecture, everything is branded as the Masterbrand. There are no sub-brands or discrete marketing properties. Instead, there are descriptors under the Masterbrand that indicate a division or business vertical. This is the most common approach for entrepreneurs and small to midsize businesses. For example, FedEx uses a Monolithic Brand Architecture. Everything is branded as FedEx, but there are descriptors under the Masterbrand to signal the different solutions offered by the FedEx brand.

Excerpt of FedEx's Monolithic Brand Architecture.

Corporation

Express

Ground

Freight

Services

Logistics

Office

Endorsed. In the Endorsed Brand Architecture, there's a Masterbrand and several sub-brands that are endorsed by the Masterbrand name. However, each brand may have its own unique look and feel, while also drawing some visual semblance from the Masterbrand. For example, Virgin has many sub-brands that leverage the Virgin brand name. In most cases, there is a visual semblance of the Masterbrand, whether it's the logotype of the Virgin brand or the color red. However, in some cases, you see unique expressions and different fonts and colors used, primarily to give a specific brand a unique feel that caters to that market.

Excerpt of Virgin's Endorsed Brand Architecture

Freestanding. In the Freestanding Brand Architecture, a Masterbrand acts as a "holding company" or the "parent brand" but does not dictate the branding or look and feel of the sub-brands. Sometimes referred to as a "House of Brands," this approach is typically used in a business-to-consumer (B2C) or a product-driven go-to-market approach, in which each brand is managed separately, usually with its own unique look and feel. For example, Proctor & Gamble is a Masterbrand, but most consumers don't buy Proctor & Gamble products. Instead, they buy the separately branded products.

Hybrid. In the Hybrid Brand Architecture, a Masterbrand acts as a "parent brand" but does not dictate the branding or look and feel of the sub-brands. However, in this case, oftentimes, the branding and look and feel of the Masterbrand is leveraged in the sub-brands, where appropriate. In other scenarios, a sub-brand may need its own unique "look and feel." For example, the Coca-Cola Company owns several brands that leverage the branding from the Coca-Cola brand, while some brands, particularly those acquired by the Coca-Cola Company, retained their own branding. Arguably, most people may not even know that some brands are owned by the parent brand.

IS YOUR BRAND ARCHITECTURE YOU OR A BUSINESS?

Shanda Sumpter is a successful business and marketing coach. When I met her, she referred to herself as "Queen Visionary" of her business "Heartcore Women." Even though she was doing remarkably well running a seven-figure business, many of her colleagues were telling her she needed to rebrand. Eventually, those conversations caught up to her and she admitted to having "brand shame," because she felt that her brand did not match her level of success and achievement. And, her brand was largely centered around her. While Shanda was a master of sales and marketing, she wanted her brand to represent an enterprise—a larger organization—rather than a one-person show like most business and marketing coaches.

But when she started working with us, she was in for a much bigger conversation than just the changing of her logo and colors. We ended up changing her company name—and eventually her Brand Architecture.

Shanda believes that you need to lead from the heart to grow your life and your business. And she was passionate about building a community of other women who believe this same philosophy. She referred to them as Heartcore Women, and so her "Masterbrand" was Heartcore Women. Many of the women who sought out Shanda were attracted to her magnetic and influential brand personality. She would continue to draw women to her because her Brand Architecture was organized around a Personal Brand.

Shanda Sumpter's Before Logo for Heartcore Women

After several hours strategizing with Shanda, I asked her, "Are you open to changing your company name?"

"Well, I'm not sure, because I *really* like the concept of Heartcore Women," she replied. She probably thought I was going to tell her to rebrand using just her name, like many of her peers in the industry.

But my counsel was different. I assured Shanda that I wasn't taking something *away* from her. Rather, I was *adding* something to her Brand Architecture. I wanted to leverage the name "Heartcore" in a more meaningful way, while simultaneously creating a Brand Architecture that positioned her brand as a real business with many sub-brands underneath it.

I continued explaining my rationale to Shanda, "Heartcore Women is a great name. Maybe it's what you call your clients. Maybe it's a sub-brand, such as a program. Or maybe it's the name of your online membership portal. I don't know yet, but I am concerned that new people won't take you seriously because you don't sound like a business. In addition, I think the name limits your ability to leverage your brand to expand into other business interests or client prospects. For example, do you really want to rule out the option of working with men? How about just shifting your company name from Heartcore Women to Heartcore Business?"

Many of us resist change, but we all know that sometimes change is necessary for a higher good. Shanda thought about it and resisted. She wasn't initially convinced. She did, however, admit that men were attracted to her coaching style. After a week, she finally confessed that it needed to change. It was the right thing to do for the future of her business.

Heartcore Business was born. This new name embodied many aspects of her work and provided a built-in naming convention for her Brand Architecture. Using the Monolithic Brand Architecture approach, we then built out other revenue streams: Heartcore Media and Heartcore Endurance. Now, her business is not just a coaching business. She established her business and brand as an entrepreneurial training company.

Shanda Sumpter's New Logo for Heartcore Business

"Through the branding process, my brand grew up and futurized," says Shanda. "The process put real meaning, direction, and structure around my brand. I upleveled as a human being. For me, being my brand feels like leverage. The company has its own personality and architecture because of the many human beings plugged into its culture."

IS YOUR BRAND ARCHITECTURE SCALABLE?

Debi Berndt Maldonado and Dr. Rob had built a successful love and relationship coaching business under the banner Sexy True Love. They intuitively knew that the brand didn't accurately represent their work, but they couldn't identify how to fix or evolve it.

I met the couple at an entrepreneurial conference that we were both sponsoring. Their booth was just a few down from mine. Debi came up to me and shared her challenge. She knew she needed to rebrand but wasn't sure how to go about doing it. I walked over to their booth and took one look at their trade show banner.

I asked, "What exactly are you selling? Romance novels?"

Debi and Dr. Rob laughed and continued the joke, "It looks like we're selling sex, right?"

The truth of the matter was Debi and Dr. Rob had in-depth experience and credentials helping people leverage Jungian philosophy to tap into the subconscious mind to find true love. They wanted to expand their work with the subconscious mind to impact more people in other areas of life and they felt their brand wasn't scalable to expand in the years to come.

When we worked with Debi and Dr. Rob, we changed their name to Creative Love which made it easier to attract the right people to the deep work that they do. This name change and shift in brand positioned them differently in the market. Their brand was not therapy. They were motivational, but not superficial. They truly were in a category of one. No one else was doing what they were doing. The reason people take their online programs is because they sound different from everything else in the relationship space.

As part of our engagement, we also developed their Brand Architecture and designed a new Visual Identity with the intention that the brand would be scalable. One important aspect of the brand was the creation of an "infinity" symbol as part of the logo. This logo—or "mark"—became a visual identifier in their Brand Architecture that anchored their brand—helping them leverage their existing brand equity in the love and relationship coaching industry (so as to not lose current clients and raving fans), while also allowing them to expand into other areas of personal development such as money, spirituality, and wellness (and attract new customers and clients).

As with many high-growth entrepreneurs, a few years later, the business grew indeed. But, the important moral of the story is that the brand was scalable to grow and evolve with the business. The original infinity symbol was leveraged as the common through line. It maintained clients' trust despite the changes in the business.

Debi and Dr. Rob's Brand Evolution

Sexy True Love	Creative Love	Debi and Dr. Rob
Love and Relationship Coaching	Love and Relationship Coaching	Personal Development Experts

Through an evolutionary process, their brand now has a scalable Brand Architecture. "Our business is now a company we can sell," says Debi. "The previous Brand

Architecture was too much, unfocused, and scattered. We were trying to be everything for everyone and spreading ourselves too thin. Having the right Brand Architecture helped us focus our message and build a brand for scale. In addition, the Brand Architecture saves us a lot of money on advertising, as opposed to spending in multiple verticals. Our open rates are increasing. We're doing less work and bringing in more income. We cut out 60 percent of our programs but make the same amount of revenue. Our Brand Architecture keeps us focused as we continue to scale-up."

IS YOUR BRAND ARCHITECTURE INCONSISTENT?

Similar to Debi and Dr. Rob, Brent Weaver had a Brand Architecture challenge. Brent, the CEO and founder of UGURUS, a business academy for web entrepreneurs and digital agencies, realized there was increasingly a disconnection between his company name, product and program offerings, and his community.

"Every one of the names for our brands and offerings has its own identity. Not only do we have our main Company Brand 'UGURUS,' but we have '10k Bootcamp' and 'Discovery Masterclass.' Then '10k' became its own thing. And, we continued to market the Bootcamps by using '10k' and then adding a location to the name, e.g., '10k Denver' and '10k Austin.' All in all, our branding was based on each individual product and not centered around a core idea. None of our offerings tied back to the main UGURUS brand."

UGUrUS

Furthermore, Brent began to question whether the story of helping web professionals become "gurus" was still relevant. As it was, the "guru" label used in the marketplace had become overused and diluted. It didn't carry the same weight and credibility as before, mainly because it seemed that countless new people in every industry had begun labeling themselves a "guru." There was something deeper and simpler for Brent, and we went on a quest to find out what that was.

During the branding process, we uncovered Brent's true mission for his business academy. Having been in the trenches much like his clientele, he knew what it was like to be overworked, undervalued, and unappreciated as a web company or digital agency that works hard for its clients. He had the foresight to see a solution in which web professionals could receive coaching advice, collaborative feedback, and be heard by a supportive community.

To represent the spirit of his mission, we recommended a new Brand Promise: "Better Together."

Rather than recommending that he change his company name altogether, we decided to shift the focal point of the word "gurus" by emphasizing the letter "U" in the name. In doing so, the story of the brand became about the mentor/mentee relationship and the community—rather than the dream of becoming a "guru."

We now had an anchor to create a consistent story across all of Brent's offerings. To help do that, we crafted a new logo that highlighted and leveraged the "U" in the brand name in a distinct way. In addition, if you look closely, you'll notice a second "U" integrated into the logo—this became a subtle way to convey the message: "Better Together." And, finally, the upward-facing, pencil-like arrows at the end of the "U" suggest two additional storylines: 1) a path towards growth and 2) a subtle reminder of education.

However, the most important aspect of the new logo is how the "U" became a visual identifier for his new Brand Architecture. We now had a way to keep consistency across his brand and sub-brands. In doing so, we renamed "10K Bootcamp" to "UCAMP." In addition, we introduced two new sub-brands: "USUMMIT" (the company's annual event) and "UACADEMY" (the company's core training program).

UGURUS

USUMMIT   UCAMP   UACADEMY

According to Brent, "Our new Brand Architecture helped us stay consistent with our branding. Our USUMMIT event grew by 300 percent, and we're able to charge four times more for our core program, UACADEMY."

IS YOUR BRAND ARCHITECTURE FRAGMENTED?

Located in Queensland's Sunshine Coast, Changing Habits was founded by wife and husband team, Cyndi and Howard O'Meara. Changing Habits is an online site that offers more than five hundred whole food products for delivery. However, their whole food products only tell half their story. As the company expanded over time, they added a nutrition training academy for people interested in starting businesses as health and nutrition mentors, and several additional health-related programs.

Cyndi and Howard also built a farm that "nurtures the soil and the microbes that live within, to create health for those that depend upon its bounty." A place where "the animals are treated with kindness, fed a natural diet free from chemicals and genetically modified foods, and allowed to enjoy an outdoor life."

As with most businesses that expand quickly, the concept of Brand Architecture is usually the last thing on their minds. The result: a fragmented brand.

To illustrate this point, here's a brief snapshot of Changing Habits' offerings.

As you can see, there's no clear integration of guidelines for how to leverage the Changing Habits brand. Instead, the approach was to just continue adding new products and programs and "make it up" as they went along. This approach is quite common among businesses but it's not their fault. They simply didn't have a systematized framework and guidelines for maintaining the integrity of their brand.

In working with the Changing Habits team, the first objective was to clarify all of their revenue streams in terms of core offerings. In doing so, we were able to better frame the business and organize the offerings into an ecosystem of brands. As you can see in the chart below, Changing Habits has two core offerings: products and programs.

In the product offering column, we decided that all products would be branded "Changing Habits," but in marketing, the products would be categorically organized under several buckets, e.g., chocolate, spices, condiments, flour and mixes, skincare, cleaning products, nutritional support.

However, the program offering column is slightly different. After reviewing the different programs, we determined that branding them under the "Changing Habits" name would not work as well in marketing. The program needed to stand out on its own and not create confusion in the marketplace. It needed to be clear that it wasn't a product. So, the goal was to determine the best way to create a relationship with Changing Habits, as the Masterbrand, in a subtle way. After careful consideration, I recommended four program categories: Lifestyle, Education, Leadership, and Impact.

Masterbrand					CHANGING HABITS			
Core Offerings	Products				Programs			
Categories	Whole Foods	Chocolate	Spices	Condiments	Lifestyle	Education	Leadership	Impact
	Flour & Mixes	Dried Fruits, Nuts, Seeds	Mueseli & Oats	Cleaning Products				
	Books & Audio	Nutritional Support	Merchandise	Skin Care				

Under this new Brand Architecture, the strategy was to use Changing Habits as an endorsement for the program brand. In doing so, this allowed the program to stand out on its own. For example, The Fat Loss Protocol program is a lifestyle program, so it now uses the endorsement "a Changing Habits lifestyle program." And, The Nutrition Academy is an educational program, so it uses the endorsement "a Changing Habits educational program." The chart below illustrates the complete Brand Architecture strategy for how the Masterbrand's look and feel now became an integrated, non-fragmented ecosystem of brands, sub-brands, and marketing properties.

Masterbrand	CHANGING HABITS			
Core Offerings	Programs			
Categories	Lifestyle	Education	Leadership	Impact
Sub Brands and Marketing Properties	The Fat Loss Protocol *a Changing Habits lifestyle program* Real Food Reset *a Changing Habits lifestyle program* 6 Weeks No Wheat *a Changing Habits lifestyle program*	The Nutrition Academy *a Changing Habits educational program*	Mastermind	Regenerative Food Production *a Changing Habits impact program* The Nutrition Alliance *a Changing Habits impact program* The Whole Foods Co-Op *a Changing Habits impact program* Collective Foundation Farm

In summary, your Brand Architecture is a strategic framework that organizes your revenue streams and offerings from a branding perspective. The benefits are twofold. First, you'll save yourself time and money by reducing or eliminating the need to duplicate branding (and design) efforts. Second, you'll leverage and optimize your marketing efforts by building an ecosystem of brands in your portfolio.

ACTION STEPS FOR AN AUTHENTIC BRAND ARCHITECTURE

1. Decide which type of Brand Architecture makes the most sense for your business.
   A. Monolithic
   B. Endorsed
   C. Freestanding
   D. Hybrid
2. Make a list of the revenue streams in your business model. Only focus on the ways your business will con-

tinue to make money in the next three to five years. For example, if you currently generate revenue primarily through services, but are transitioning to a 100 percent product-based business, then don't list "Services" as part of your revenue streams.

3. Organize the revenue streams into one to five broad buckets or categories. For example:
   A. Products
   B. Services
   C. Programs
   D. Events
   E. Commission
   F. Subscription/Membership

Note: You may find that your revenue fits into multiple categories. If that's the case, put the revenue in a primary category. For example, if you only sell products on a subscription basis, simply categorize them under "Subscription." But if you sell products both on a non-subscription and subscription basis, organize them under "Products" in which there will be two subcategories: "Non-subscription" and "Subscription."

4. Finally, based on your chosen Brand Architecture AND the relationship each revenue stream will need to have with the Masterbrand, organize your revenue streams under the new framework and develop guidelines as to how you'll name and brand each type of revenue stream. For example:

A. Is it branded under the Masterbrand? Then a descriptor for the "solution" or "division" is needed.
B. Is it endorsed by the Masterbrand, using the Masterbrand name and another branded product name?
C. Is it endorsed by the Masterbrand, in a subtle way, e.g., "powered by...?"
D. Is it a freestanding brand that has its own look and feel devoid of the Masterbrand?

Building a Brand, Authentically

CHAPTER NINE

The Science of the Branding Process

METHOD TO THE MADNESS

"Can you just create a quick logo for me?"

I was on a sales call with a prospect who wanted to work with my firm, and this was his opening question. I politely and confidently declined his request. It's not that I didn't want to help this person, it's just that it's irresponsible for me to promise a great logo without the strategic brand thinking behind it. This philosophical point of departure is core to what I believe as a branding professional. In fact, one of the biggest differentiators between a branding professional and a designer is the ability to not only think creatively, but also to think strategically from a business and marketing perspective. Generally speaking, a designer leads with how beautiful a brand looks. However, a branding professional leads with how design needs to align with the ethos of the brand, while at the same time, enabling the company to optimize its marketing objectives.

The combination of strategic and creative thinking is exactly why branding is a blend of *both* art and science. I'd take it even further and say that if you approach branding with only the design perspective (art), it's only partially authentic, and, therefore, partially inauthentic. Conversely, if you approach branding with only the analytical and strategic (science) perspective, it's also partially authentic, and thus partially inauthentic. Keep in mind that because of this blend of art and science the process will sometimes feel linear and other times it will feel nonlinear.

Clearly, the entire premise of this book is about creating more authenticity in your brand. That said, if you truly want an authentic brand, I believe you'll need to build your brand...*authentically*. The starting point *isn't* the art, it's the science. The chart below outlines my signature three-phase process that I've harnessed and simplified over my branding career.

The Branding For The People Three-Phase Branding Process.

The "Science"	The "Art"	The "Art and Science"
Phase One: Brand Strategy	Phase Two: Brand Identity	Phase Three: Brand Marketing
Building the brand foundation to deliver on the business goals.	Create the guidelines and assets for the brand look, feel and voice.	Design and produce the high-priority brand and marketing touchpoints.

In this chapter, we'll unpack the "Science" of the branding process.

PHASE ONE: BRAND STRATEGY

What is a Brand Strategy? Let's start with the term "strategy" (the elusive, intangible term that most people don't grasp). Merriam-Webster's definition of strategy is "a careful plan or method for achieving a particular goal usually over a long period of time." If you're committed to building a brand over time...the question becomes: Why would you NOT have a Brand Strategy?

You most likely have a business strategy. You may even have a marketing strategy. But what sits in-between both is your Brand Strategy. Skipping ahead to marketing strategy without having Brand Strategy is the mistake most business owners make. Brand Strategy is the first step to building a brand, because it builds the foundation and guides all downstream decisions and activities. Your Brand Strategy defines and articulates several layers of your brand including: Target Audiences, Brand Purpose, Brand Archetypes, Brand Architecture, the competitive landscape, Brand Promise, Brand Positioning, Brand Platform, and Messaging.

TARGET AUDIENCES

Regardless if you're a large, established enterprise or a one-person entrepreneur, branding is an outside-in approach, which means starting with your target audiences before anything else. Specifically, you'll need to answer the "Who, What, Why" questions:

1. Who are your target audiences?
2. What are the problems you solve for your target audiences?
3. Why should your target audiences listen to, buy from, or recommend you?

Who are your target audiences?

In chapter one, you learned the story of the Tiffany and Walmart branded eighteen-karat-gold earrings. Remember that, compared to the unbranded earrings, the students were willing to pay 65 percent more for the Tiffany brand. Whereas, the students were willing to pay 85 percent less for the Walmart brand. The same pair of eighteen-karat-gold earrings will command different pricing, because each brand has different answers to the "Who, What, Why" questions.

To paint a full picture of your target audiences it's important to define both the demographic details and the psychographic profile. For further clarification, demographic details refer to factors such as age, race, gender, income, and location. Demographics don't tell you everything, but they are a great place to start. To dig deeper, you'll want to understand your target audiences' psychographic profile, which refers to their fears, frustrations, wants and aspirations, personality traits, lifestyle patterns, interests, attitudes and purchasing behaviors. This profile is arguably more important than demographics.

Here are two examples of psychographic profiles:

Example: Target Audiences for a Real Estate Broker

Recent Newlyweds	Wealthy Retirees	Busy Career Professional
Decent credit score	Great credit score	Great credit score
No assets and no debt	Lots of assets	No assets
First-time homebuyer for primary residence	Primary residence in country/suburbs	High income salary
		Renter looking to buy
Needs space for one to two kids	Looking for a *pied-à-terre*	Needs a modern loft for an easy commute

Example: Target Audiences for a Credit Card Company

Transactor	Revolver	Arbitrager	Non-User	Deadbeats
Uses card frequently	Uses card frequently	Games system to make or save money	Keeps zero balance	Uses card until blocked
Pays in full every time	Carries debt each month	Leverages zero percent balance transfers	Uses for emergency only	Never pays on time
Avoids paying interest rates	Pays the minimum or a little above		Maintains credit history	Doesn't have intention of paying back
Gathers points		Usually has multiple credit cards		

Together, demographics and psychographics help you better understand your target audiences and build a brand that resonates with them.

What are the problems you solve for your target audiences?

All businesses and brands should solve people's problems. Knowing the problems you solve will also inform your messaging and go-to-market approach. Think of the problems you solve as fitting under three broad categories:

Example: Eighteen-karat-gold earrings

	Functional	Economic	Emotional
	Measured in terms of usefulness or utility	Measured in terms of time or money	Measured in terms of feelings or aspirations
Walmart	"Complements my outfit"	"Fashion on a budget"	"I look pretty"
Tiffany	"Is the appropriate and perfect anniversary gift"	"It's a precious investment"	"I'm making a statement about my status"

Why should your target audiences listen to, buy from, or recommend you?

Your target audiences are increasingly savvy and skeptical, so you have to be smart about how you appeal to them. Customers are becoming poised to distrust. To overcome and address this, you'll need to clearly articulate the core "Proof Points" that either lend or establish your credibility as a brand to trust. Proof Points are simply that—"proof" that you or your company is trustworthy and credulous.

Broad statements make you sound untrustworthy. Clarify your Proof Points with specificity. Rather than saying, "we've spoken at hundreds of conferences," you would say, "our six advisors have collectively spoken at fourteen hundred conferences over the past ten years." If you don't have any Proof Points, you'll need to work on building them, because you'll find it more difficult to ask a prospective buyer to simply "trust you" with no evidence that you can solve their problems. If you do convince a customer or client to trust you without Proof Points make sure you deliver—rather, overdeliver—on your promises so that you can start to build tangible Proof Points for future clients.

If you're unsure what constitutes a Proof Point, below is a chart with examples to help you understand the range of evidence you can use to articulate *why* your target audiences should listen to, buy from, or recommend you. While this is not an all-inclusive list, you'll want to pay attention to which Proof Points influence your target audience's decision to buy from you.

Example: Proof Points

Business or Profession	Proof Point Type	Proof Point Example
Media Mogul	Origin Story/Anecdote	Born into poverty, the first non-white TV correspondent
Business Consultant	Client List	Former CEO of Fortune 500 brands
Men's Coach	Experience	25+ years of coaching thousands of men around the world
Online Education Company	Statistics	95 percent course completion rate
Marketing Influencer	Social Proof	1.5 million followers on Facebook and Instagram
Personal Trainer	Certifications	Certification from International Sports Scientists Association
Shoe Manufacturer	Celebrity Endorsements	Michael Jordan's Nike shoes
Consumer Products	Reviews	5-star ratings on Amazon
Motivational Speaker	Media	As seen on NBC, CBS, and ABC
Acting Coach	Awards	5-time Academy Award Winner

BRAND PURPOSE

Once you're clear on the "Who, What, Why" of your target audiences, the next step is to use that information to define your Brand Purpose. Your Brand Purpose is written in the form of a statement and provides a beacon of light for why the company exists and the direction the company is headed. While there are many styles to a Brand Purpose statement, here are some general guidelines I use for crafting a powerful Brand Purpose statement:

1. Make sure it answers the question "why does this brand exist?"
2. Keep it to twenty-one words or less.
3. Write it in the personality and voice of the brand.
4. You might include your target audiences, industry, or category.
5. You might include your core solutions, offerings, or the problems you solve.
6. Make sure it evokes an emotion or aspiration.

Example: Big Companies' Brand Purpose Statements

Amazon	Patagonia	Whole Foods
To offer our customers the lowest possible prices, the best available selection, and the utmost convenience.	To build the best product, cause no unnecessary harm, use business to inspire and implement solutions to the environmental crisis.	To nourish people and the planet.

Example: Small Businesses' Brand Purpose Statements

Company	Brand Purpose
Changing Habits (whole food company)	We are influencing how our food is produced, classified and marketed.
Syntratech (supplement company)	For people with diabetes, we bring a radical, non-pharma approach for normalizing blood glucose.
Amazing (training company for Amazon sellers)	We make amazing lives possible by helping entrepreneurial people build their brands on Amazon.
The Mimic Method (online language learning company)	We are the first truly effective language learning program that helps people break through cultural barriers.
PurpleCare (landscaping, lawn care, pest control company)	We are here to create stronger, harder-working, friendlier, and more beautiful communities, from the ground up.
Thorben (cloud tech company)	We turn IT headaches into profit-growth systems for organizations who are working to make the world more extraordinary.

BRAND ARCHETYPES

Archetypes are a concept originally conceived by famed Swiss psychiatrist, Carl Jung. When used in branding and marketing, the concept is referred to as Brand Archetypes. Essentially, Brand Archetypes are used by branding professionals as a heuristic to infuse personality into a company's brand. When creating your Brand Strategy, we recommend identifying one or two Brand Archetypes. A Brand Archetype is identified when you fill in the blank to the following statement: If our company were a person, that person would be described as _____. It's important to identify your

Brand Archetypes based on where the brand is heading (not where the brand has historically been).

BRAND ARCHITECTURE

As discussed in chapter eight, Brand Architecture is "a strategic framework that organizes your offerings and determines how to brand (or not brand) them from both a verbal and visual perspective." Remember, there are four broad frameworks for Brand Architecture: Monolithic, Endorsed, Freestanding, and Hybrid. Your Brand Architecture is determined in the Brand Strategy phase, and provides guidance for your design team to create a Visual Identity that integrates your Masterbrand, sub-brands, and marketing properties.

COMPETITIVE REVIEW

Depending on your appetite to understand your competitors, you'll want to conduct a review of three to seven competitors. The sweet spot is your top five competitors. This process is relatively easy as it involves primarily desk research, i.e., researching your competitors on their website, social media, and other marketing channels. There are six key competitor elements to explore:

Visual	Verbal
What does their logo look like?	What do they seem to talk most about?
For example, nonexistent, dated, innovative, fresh, or boring.	*For example, messaging is primarily focused on making money, living the dream, and enjoying your lifestyle.*
What colors do they use?	What does the voice of their brand sound like?
For example, competitors all seem to use earthy green and other earth tone colors.	*For example, funny, academic, serious.*
How would you describe the overall look and feel of their branding/designs?	What seems to be their overall Brand Positioning?
For example, overall designs look cutting edge, masculine and sophisticated.	*For example, positioning is upscale and exclusive OR position is mass-market and inclusive.*

BRAND POSITIONING

After you have a clear understanding of the competitive landscape, now it's time to find the "white space" in your industry or category. This helps you determine your Brand Positioning. In simple terms, your Brand Positioning is the space that you occupy (or intend to occupy) in your target audiences' minds. It helps to distinguish or differentiate your company from your competitors.

There are many ways to "position" your brand. There's not just one way, but it's critical that your Brand Promise is articulated based on your Brand Positioning.

Here are some examples of how big companies position their brands:

Example: Positioning around a Word or Concept

Volvo	Jeep	BMW
Safety	Rugged	The Ultimate Driving Machine

Example: Positioning Through Color

Verizon	AT&T	T-Mobile	Sprint
Red	Blue	Pink	Yellow

Example: Positioning around Time

Debeers	Geico	FedEx
A diamond is forever.	15 minutes can save you 15 percent or more.	The World On Time.

To help find the white space in your industry, create a Brand Positioning Map. A Brand Positioning Map enables you to visualize how your brand is unique in the competitive landscape.

To illustrate how it works, I'll show my company's Brand Positioning Map. When I left the big branding firms, I needed to visualize a Brand Positioning Map that outlined how my company is distinct from other branding agencies or resources. There are two axes to the chart. The x-axis represents branding agencies that target "Fortune 500 companies" versus "small to midsize businesses." The y-axis represents branding agencies that are *"strategic and holistic"* versus *"tactical or specialized."*

Brand Positioning Map for Branding For The People

Strategic & Holistic

Interbrand   FutureBrand

Landor   LIPPINCOTT   Branding For The People.

+ siegel gale   WOLFF OLINS

Fortune 500 Companies ←———————————————→ Small-to-Midsize Businesses

Pentagram   fiverr°

bluemarlin   upwork

DigitasLBi   99designs

HUGE   Business coaches
Marketing consultants
Graphic designers
razorfish   Digital marketers
Social media experts

Tactical or Specialized

For your Brand Positioning Map, you'll need to determine the two axes that frame the key aspects of your competitive environment. Here are some examples of axes to help you brainstorm the spectrums in your Brand Positioning Map:

- Quality (low vs. high) and Quantity (minimum vs. maximum)
- Speed (slow vs. fast) and Efficacy (poor vs. excellent)
- Relationship (transactional vs. family-oriented) and Delivery method (freight delivery vs. white glove service)
- Food (fast casual vs. fine dining) and Location (everywhere vs. select locations)

- Fitness activity (inactive vs. active) and Nutrition approach (regimented vs. flexible)

BRAND PROMISE

The next step after you've identified your Brand Positioning is to articulate your Brand Promise. Your Brand Promise is the ultimate benefit that your customers or clients will receive when they buy your products or services. It guides everything about your brand, from how you look, to how you speak, and to the customer experience.

Examples: Brand Promise Statements

Nike	Google	Uber
To bring inspiration and innovation to every athlete.	To be the world's number one source of information.	Moving people to where they want to be. In their day, in their lives, in the moment.

I recommend articulating your Brand Promise in fourteen words or less. The shorter the better. The reason? When your Brand Promise is concise, it's easy to remember. And memorability is key in branding. Plus it will be easier to implement. So, have fun wordsmithing your Brand Promise to get it just perfect. Avoid lengthy Brand Promise statements in an attempt to include everything. You don't need to put the responsibility on your Brand Promise to communicate everything. You'll have other areas, such as Messaging, to express different aspects of your brand.

That said, the most important thing is to make sure that your Brand Promise fulfills the following three criteria:

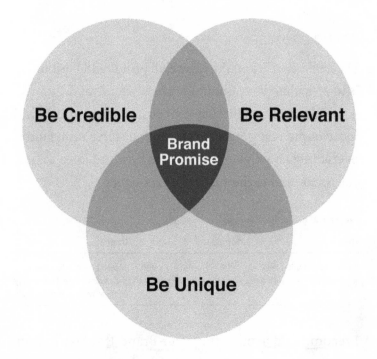

Criteria One: Be Credible

The first criteria is that your Brand Promise must be credible. In other words, your Brand Promise has to be something you can support with evidence or proof. You don't want to claim something that has no substance or that is difficult to prove.

Let's play this out using a "life coach." Let's say that this particular life coach is a nineteen-year-old, bright young man. Perhaps he's gone through one or two life transformations. His Brand Promise is centered around coaching and empowering forty-five- to fifty-year-old women who want to break through a midlife crisis. Can he credibly own this Brand Promise? Is he even a credible person for this target market? It's not impossible, but I would think twice about hiring him if I was the target audience. How much life wisdom can he truly provide to older women?

Criteria Two: Be Relevant

The second criteria is that your Brand Promise must be relevant to your target audiences. Earlier in this chapter, we explained how to understand deeply your target audiences, by answering the questions: Who, What, and Why? You can identify areas to be relevant by reviewing the answers to the question: "What are the problems you solve for your target audiences?" See if there's an overarching problem or a theme to all the problems that you solve.

Another way to explore how to be relevant to your target audiences is to use a framework I call "The Relevancy Matrix." This matrix illustrates two scales. The horizontal scale goes from "Opposing Values" to "Aligned Values" and the vertical scale goes from "High Impact" to "Low Impact."

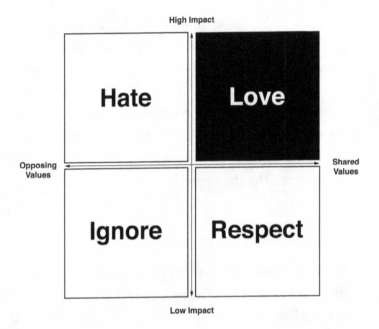

High Impact

Hate

Love

Opposing Values

Shared Values

Ignore

Respect

Low Impact

Brands We Love

These brands are strongly aligned with our values and they make a positive impact on our lives. They solve our problems and provide solutions. These are the brands that we love and the ones that we gladly and willingly buy from. We become evangelists for these brands, and we tell the world about them.

Brands We Respect

These brands are also strongly aligned with our own values, but they have a low impact on our lives. Maybe they don't solve our everyday problems or offer solutions that aren't relevant to us right now. But, if we need them, we're likely to buy these brands because we already hold great respect for them.

Brands We Hate

On the opposite side of brands we love are brands we hate. These brands have a high impact on our lives, but in a *negative* way. Their values are in direct opposition to our own. We don't agree with their point-of-view, and we're most likely never going to buy from these brands. We wish we could ignore them, but we can't. In fact, we may even love to hate these brands.

Brands We Ignore

The brands in the lower left quadrant have little to no impact on our lives—positively or negatively. Their values are not in alignment with our own. They're in a neutral zone because they don't solve any of our problems. We are blind to them and we simply ignore them.

Hopefully, with this matrix, it's clear that the way to be most relevant to your target audiences is by focusing on solving the problems that, when you do, your target audiences will LOVE you for doing so.

You'll see that fitting into the upper right quadrant is the best option to become relevant to your target audiences. You're making an impact on their lives, i.e., solving their problems, and you're aligning with them based on your core beliefs and values.

Criteria Three: Be Unique

The first criteria focused on being credible by looking *within* you and inside the company. The second criteria focused on being relevant by looking at your target audiences and what will make them love you. The third criteria focuses on being unique by looking at your competitors and finding out what makes you different than everyone else. Here is where you want to express your company's "secret sauce" or most differentiating factor—whether it's a feature, a benefit, a methodology, or something else. As entrepreneur Barbara Corcoran says, "If you don't have big breasts, put ribbons on your pigtails."

In summary, your Brand Promise should not focus on one criterion over another. It's at the intersection of all three criteria where the magic happens. In a cluttered, noisy, competitive marketplace, with everyone walking around with short attention spans, a successful Brand Promise fulfills all three criteria: Be Credible, Be Relevant, and Be Unique. When your Brand Promise accomplishes all three, it will position you powerfully in the marketplace.

BRAND PLATFORM

Once you've identified your Brand Promise, the next step is to dimensionalize it into four key components: Brand Values, Brand Attributes, Brand Voice, and Value Proposition.

Components of a Brand Platform

	Definition	Tips
Brand Values	The guiding principles of behavior that deliver on the brand.	Brand Values are distinct from your personal or core values, such as integrity, honesty, trust, or customer focus, and are considered table stakes. Your personal or core values may overlap with your Brand Values; however, the important distinction is that Brand Values are specific to your company's brand.
Brand Attributes	The personality characteristics of the brand.	These personality characteristics should complement the chosen Brand Archetype(s). Typically, Brand Attributes are adjectives. If you're not sure of the wording of Brand Attributes, ask yourself if you would use that word to describe a person's personality.
Brand Voice	The sound of the brand as expressed in verbal language.	Brand Voice is useful for a copywriter to verbalize the tone and manner in which copy needs to be written. If you're not sure if the wording of the Brand Voice works, ask yourself if you would use that word to describe how a person sounds when he/she speaks.
Value Propositions	The key day-to-day tangible or intangible benefits that the brand provides.	Intangible or tangible benefits could range from functional, to economic, to emotional. Refer back to the Target Audiences section that defines each of these terms. However, instead of referring to them as problems, you're referring to the Value Propositions as benefits or solutions.

MESSAGING MATRIX

Messaging is a funny word, right? It's not often used by the general public, but it's a common word in the branding and marketing industry. The term "messaging" is basically "an organizing framework for all the messages to be used in branding and marketing communications." To explain, the word "message" is simply "a key communication point." These aren't necessarily the actual words you'll use. The messages are the crux of your communication point when you strip down all the words surrounding your point.

Here are some examples of messages:

- Safety
- Reliability
- Accessibility
- Expertise
- Social Impact

I like to call this organizing framework a "Messaging Matrix" because it segments messages according to how you, your marketing team, or your copywriter will need to use it.

There are many ways to slice and dice your Messaging Matrix. The most common way entrepreneurs and small businesses organize their message is by target audience or by hierarchy of information. In some cases, both. In either case, when your Messaging Matrix segments your messages by target audiences, it keeps you focused on communicating the right messages to the right people, based on what's most important for each. Different messages resonate with different people.

When your Messaging Matrix segments your messages by hierarchy of information, this allows you to prioritize your messages as primary, secondary, and tertiary. In this approach, all messages are important to your target audiences, but you're presenting the messages to them in the order in which they need to hear them (to help them make a buying decision). On an implementation level, when you create this hierarchy of information, you're able to identify which messages go in a headline, as a sub headline, or in the actual body copy.

In some cases, a Messaging Matrix segments messages by both target audiences and hierarchy. Here's a chart for illustrative purposes:

Example: Messaging Matrix

	Customer	Channel Partner	Potential Employee
Primary Messages	Safety	Brand Exposure	Flexible PTO
	Reliability	Shared Revenue Potential	Meaningful Work
	Customer Service		Upward mobility
		High Profile Existing Channel Partners	
Secondary Messages	Expertise	Dedicated Team	401k
	Loyalty Programs	Robust Partner Program	Global Offices
	Money-Back Guarantee		Professional Development Programs
Tertiary Messages	Social Impact	Future Partner Programs	Ranked on Most Reputable Companies
	Great Place to Work	Social Responsibility Foundation	Founder's Story
	Partner Brands		

Finally, it's important to clarify how a Messaging Matrix will be used in practice. Remember, in the Brand Strategy phase, you're defining how you want and need to be perceived. We're creating the rules, guidelines, and parameters to focus your branding efforts. The Messaging Matrix is a tool that's used in marketing, specifically when it comes to writing copy (or content).

Copy is the actual word or words used to express your messages. It's the specific words you use on your website, social media, and all branding and marketing communications. If you've ever hired or worked with a copywriter, you know that you need to tell them what you want to communicate.

Your Messaging Matrix guides them on what to say and to whom. Here are a few examples to demonstrate the difference between message and copy:

Message	Copy
Safety	We save X number of lives each year because of our state-of-the-art safety features.
Reliability	You can count on our customer service team to be there 24 hours a day, 7 days a week.
Accessibility	If you can't find what you're looking for online, schedule an in-person meeting with one of our technicians.

CREATIVE BRIEF

If you take the time to follow the steps outlined previously, you can get pretty far in defining your Brand Promise and Brand Platform—the science part of the process. When it comes to the "art" part of the process, most business owners will want to hire someone to develop a logo, typeface, and color scheme. Unless you have a creative or design skillset, you'll want to leave the creative work for creative professionals.

However, before you or your creative team can begin working on the next phase—Brand Identity—you'll need to write a proper Creative Brief, which is where the science of branding starts to merge with the art of branding. Your Brand Strategy needs to be translated into terms that a creative professional will understand—whether it's a Visual

Identity designer or a copywriter. For example, you can't go to a designer and say, "make my brand look cool" or "I'll know it when I see it." These types of instructions inevitably create endless rounds of iterations and inefficient use of creative thinking. Why? Because words, such as "cool," can be translated in many different ways—what's "cool" to you, may not be "cool" to other people.

A Creative Brief helps you make the subjective aspects of design preferences less subjective. Rather than just listing your own personal desires, the Creative Brief creates some parameters based on the strategic elements that are important to your brand.

There are key components of a Creative Brief.

Creative Criteria

Creative Criteria is a fancy way of saying the "set of principles used to evaluate and judge design, above and beyond a creative translation of the Brand Platform." For example, creative criteria might be:

- Must appeal to both entrepreneurs and corporate executives.
- Incorporate both masculine and feminine tone and energy.
- Must convey a sense of fun and playfulness.

- Demonstrates a global, international vibe (not a local, regional company).
- Is fresh, modern, and contemporary.
- Has an innovative, "tech-y" feel, without being sterile or boring.

Inspiration Branding, Logos, or Websites

To bring out the most creative, compelling, and distinct Visual Identity, I recommend gathering inspiration from brands that are outside of your industry. However, it's not uncommon to pick inspiration brands inside your industry. The only challenge with picking an industry brand is that you run the risk of becoming a "me-too" or "look-alike" brand.

Another place to look for inspiration brands are in those companies that you feel embody your chosen Brand Archetypes and the Brand Attributes identified in your Brand Platform. I recommend three to five inspiration brands. Then, when you've selected your inspiration brands, write one to two sentences for each that describe what you love about the brand. For example: Is it the colors? The photography style? The cleanliness and use of white space? The big use of type? The logo type? Or something else.

To illustrate the power of looking outside of your industry for inspiration, let's look at the invention of Listerine Breath

Strips (now called PocketPaks). We're all familiar with the liquid version of the product, but Pfizer went outside of the mouthwash industry to find inspiration for this innovative product. You may not be familiar with this, but as a kid I recall visiting the local Asian market where I'd find a favorite treat, Botan rice candy. It was such a fun experience to pop this piece of candy in my mouth because I would marvel at how the sweet rice paper slowly dissolved to nothing. If you take the idea of thin rice paper and merge it with mouthwash, you get Listerine Breath Strips.

Let's look at another example. The founders of Equinox Fitness hated workout facilities that smelled like gyms. The smell of sweat ruined the mood, so they looked at the spa industry for inspiration. Which led to creating an environment in which members enjoy an entire brand experience. Onsite you'll find a café, a spa with treatment rooms, and workout classes. Equinox doesn't even call themselves a gym, instead they refer to themselves as a "fitness club." And, to them, fitness is a lifestyle. Today, the fitness club continues to expand, and members are lining up to join this exclusive lifestyle club.

If you want to be more creative and innovative than your competitive counterparts, adopt the mindset of venturing outside of your industry for ideas that you can infuse into your brand. You just might surprise yourself in the resulting creative expression.

Color Considerations

In general, it's best to leave color selection to the design experts who have an in-depth knowledge of color theory and color psychology. However, this is also when you specify to your branding partner whether or not there are colors that you absolutely hate or absolutely love. You can also indicate if your brand must include a particular color for symbolic, cultural, or other industry-related reasons. You may have a personal preference for primary colors over pastel colors. Muted colors over jewel tones. Unless you have specific requests with regards to color, leave the entire color palette open to the designer for extensive color exploration.

Logotype Considerations

Similar with color considerations, I recommend leaving the logotype considerations in the hands of the Visual Identity experts, but you're more than welcome to communicate a logotype preference. For example, do you prefer wordmark logos? Symbol or icon-based marks? Or, a combination of the two? Below are some examples of logotypes.

Icon	Wordmark	Lettermark	Emblem	Combination
	facebook	DKNY	HARVARD UNIVERSITY	Microsoft
	NETFLIX	3M	PORSCHE	AT&T
	Uber	hp	(Starbucks)	airbnb
(Nike swoosh)	ebay	CNN	HARLEY-DAVIDSON MOTOR CYCLES	TESLA
(Mercedes)	wework	HBO	BMW	WORDPRESS

Instead of dictating what you want your Visual Identity to look like—from the logo, colors, and graphic elements—I recommend empowering your branding partner with the creative freedom and flexibility to deliver a Visual Identity that makes the most strategic sense for your brand. If you decide to work with a branding partner or even just a Visual Identity designer, remember that they are the experts, so let them do what you hired them to do—provide you options that you probably would not have ideated on your own.

Brand Implementation Plan

I recommend that every brand launch be communicated effectively to your target audiences in the channel in which they're most likely going to experience your brand. As such, Brand Implementation Planning helps to prioritize and organize the various brand touchpoints, marketing channels, brand-building activities, and internal/external resources needed to effectively implement your brand in the marketplace. A process that I like to use to accomplish this is mapping your brand touchpoints under the three key phases of brand implementation:

- Pre-launch: What needs to happen *before* launching the new brand?
- Launch: What needs to happen on Day One of the launch of the new brand?
- Post-launch: What needs to happen *after* the brand launch to maintain and sustain momentum?

Example: Brand Implementation Plan

Pre-launch			Launch	Post-launch
Month 1	Month 2	Month 3	Months 4-5	Months 6-9
Build temporary website	Train internal team on new brand	Set up launch celebration day	Conduct Day One Announcement	Continue to engage existing clients
Create teaser campaign	Train design team on brand guidelines and assets	Schedule press release	Send email blast	Initiate new marketing funnels with new branding
Update all case studies		Finalize website testing	Begin Facebook/social media campaign	
	Brief agency partners	Launch new site	Facilitate an internal team brand launch celebration	Update membership site
		Change all social media platforms		Integrate brand into sales process
			Celebrate brand launch with current clients and prospects	Align brand with HR and organizational policies and procedures
			Continue social media campaigns	

In summary, the "science" part of the branding process is your Brand Strategy. Document all the "thinking work" you've done in this phase into a Brand Strategy presentation that can be shared internally with your team and any third-party partners who will be responsible for implementing your brand. The outline of your Brand Strategy document should include the following components that were explained in this chapter:

- Target Audiences
- Brand Purpose
- Brand Archetypes
- Brand Architecture

- Competitive Review
- Brand Positioning Map and Brand Promise
- Brand Values, Brand Attributes, Brand Voice
- Value Propositions
- Messaging Matrix
- Creative Brief
- Brand Implementation Plan

At this point we've used science to compile the layers of your brand. This collected information will paint an image of your brand that can be replicated both internally and externally.

In the next chapter, we'll discuss the "art" of the branding process—your Brand Identity.

CHAPTER TEN

The Art of the Branding Process

TOO MANY COOKS IN THE KITCHEN

"Please email me your Brand Identity presentation a week before our meeting so that I can review the options in advance."

My design team and I were in the middle of the creative process of creating a Brand Identity for a major client, and this was the CEO's request in his email. It's no surprise, like most CEOs, that he had a strong personality and he wanted to control every aspect of the creative process. I'm not intimidated by people with strong personalities. In fact, some people have told me that I, too, have a strong personality. However, when you're hiring a professional who's an expert in their field, my advice is to allow them to do what you've hired them to do, especially if branding or design is not your bailiwick.

When I read the email, I was busy participating in an event where I had just finished a keynote presentation. Rather than just replying with a simple "no," I replied with a friendly but direct explanation.

"Unfortunately, that won't work. We do not email our creative work until after we've had the opportunity to present it over a call. Furthermore, the directions we're crafting are not fully developed. In case you were wondering, we're currently fleshing out five directions, but we still need to shortlist and refine our options to deliver three of the strongest directions. Remember, you hired us to be your branding partner. Don't worry, you'll be wowed by the options we're cooking up for you!"

A move to send our designs mid-development would completely derail the integrity of our process. The designs were not complete, and he would be reviewing half-baked directions. We didn't want him to form opinions before our recommended directions had been completely thought through on our end.

I'm prepared for it to being judged that my response was not "client-friendly." In my career, I have found that clients appreciated me more for challenging them to think bigger and delivering a Brand Identity that made the most strategic sense for the business—not how "nice" or "friendly" I was in the creative development process.

When you hire a branding partner, I strongly believe you should hand over creative freedom to imagine the best Brand Identity for your business. Ostensibly, you'll find that the end result will surpass what you could imagine on your own. Just as you wouldn't tell an Executive Chef how to cook your meal or check-in midway if your meal is on track to being delicious, I encourage you not to meddle in the creative process.

If you recall earlier in the book, I shared a story about Nick Unsworth and his brand "Life on Fire." There's another part to his story—the one where we almost fired each other. You see, Nick was one of those clients who liked to "come into the kitchen" regularly, using our chef metaphor. When it came time to work on his Brand Identity, he was adamant that his logo include a blue flame. He believed that it would be a logo people would want to "tattoo" on their bodies.

I challenged him and asked, "Why do you want a blue flame in the logo? You already have a brand name Life on Fire. Do you really need to have a logo with a blue flame? Not only would a flame be predictable and literal, but it may not be the best option for your Brand Identity. "

"Furthermore, " I said, "the criteria of a logo that could easily "be tattooed" is subject to interpretation. Everyone has different tastes in tattoos. You came to me because you wanted to build a million-dollar brand. But, my vision for you is to build a ten-million-dollar brand."

Luckily, Nick backed down. We didn't fire each other. He conceded to place his trust in me and the creative process. I assured him that our end goals were aligned and that I wouldn't let him down.

Not everyone has a creative, artistic, or design sense. In fact, I can think of a few clients during my career who clearly had bad taste in design. Through no fault of their own, design was not their thing. They were more left-brained, literal thinkers. If you have poor design sense, chances are you're hiring a branding partner for their good taste. For your own good, put your ego aside when working with a branding partner and give up creative control to them.

Yes, high-performing entrepreneurs and demanding small business CEOs, this section is especially for you!

I recognize that you've had to wear many hats to get to where you are, but now it's time to retire some of the hats and let others wear them for you. If you truly want to take your brand to an entirely new level, collaborate with your branding partner. Don't dictate and mandate.

PHASE TWO: BRAND IDENTITY

The art of the branding process begins with the creation of a company's Brand Identity. More than just a logo, a Brand Identity is comprised of two components: a Visual Identity (i.e., logo, color palette, typography style, photography style, graphic elements) and a Verbal Identity (i.e., style, tone, manner, voice). While each branding partner has their own methodology, I'll briefly explain the protocol that my firm follows to create a Brand Identity.

MOOD BOARDS

Before exploring a Visual Identity direction, we start with translating the Brand Platform and Creative Brief into three different mood boards. This step allows you to further narrow down the desired visual look and feel of your brand. A "Mood Board" is a collection of images (photography, graphics, type/fonts) coordinated to create a visual language with a distinct "tone" and "feeling." It is not a collection of images to be used literally. It's not recommended photography. And, if there are words in the Mood Board, they're usually there to represent a typography style and feel (not the specific message of the words).

Here are three Mood Board examples for my client Hunter+Esquire, an executive search firm specializing in placing top talent in the cannabis industry. The objective in showing three mood boards is to provide options to the client and identify the one mood board that will be used to advance to the next step.

VISUAL IDENTITY DIRECTIONS

Based on the chosen Mood Board, now it's time to explore two or three different Visual Identity directions. I recommend that your branding partner show the Visual Identity directions by illustrating the logo/mark, color palette, typography style, photography style, and all graphic elements that would likely be part of the visual system. I also encourage them to illustrate the brand in different touchpoints, such as a T-shirt, billboard, product packaging, trade show banner (or other relevant brand touchpoint).

Below you'll see the three Visual Identity directions for Hunter+Esquire, based on Mood Board 03:

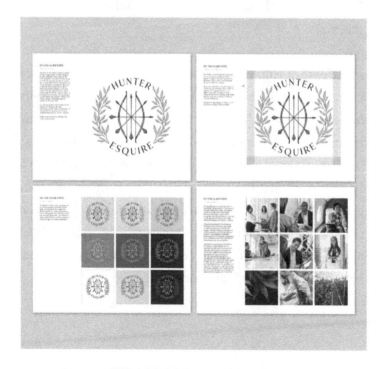

In this step, it's quite common to go through an iterative process by making adjustments and refinement to the chosen Visual Identity direction. You want to provide clear feedback and direction to your branding partner as to what you love and what you don't love about the chosen direction. Be specific with feedback on the logo itself, colors, typography, and even the overall look and feel of the brand.

If you're not a creative person and don't understand design and art, it might be useful to evaluate the Visual Identity directions by referring back to the Brand Platform and the Creative Criteria. Ask yourself: Does the Visual Identity direction represent the elements of the Brand Platform? Does the Visual Identity direction fulfill on the creative criteria?

In the case of Hunter+Esquire, the client wanted to explore cannabis leaves (instead of laurel leaves) and other fonts besides the one chosen in the original direction. This is absolutely acceptable. Sometimes one of two things happen: 1) you'll end up loving the refinement, or 2) you'll be confident that the original direction is the better solution. The image below shows the original version of the Hunter+Esquire logo, the various iterations, and the final approved output. Through collaboration and clear feedback, we arrived at a logo that everyone loved.

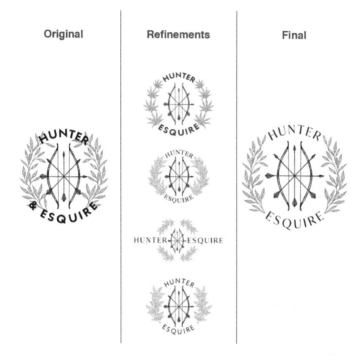

Original	Refinements	Final

VERBAL IDENTITY

In addition to a Visual Identity, we recommend developing a Verbal Identity. Verbal Identity is a powerful way to ensure that the brand speaks in the same voice across all marketing and communication channels.

Verbal Identity determines the language used inside an organization. For example, Starbucks refers to their cup sizes as Tall, Grande, and Venti, as opposed to Small, Medium, and Large. Disney refers to its staff as "cast members," not "employees." And, Apple branded their support department by calling it the "Genius Bar."

When you are clear on your brand, your brand gives you the tone in which to speak. It's also clear how not to speak. For example, there are different ways to greet someone in a salutation in a marketing newsletter. One brand might say, "Hey, what's up?" Another brand might say "Heya." A third brand might be more formal and say, "Dear Colleagues."

The analogy I regularly share is related to the marketing guru, Gary Vaynerchuk, who, as we've talked about, is known for his raw, bold tone with prominent usage of cursing. Everyone knows that about him. It's part of his Brand Voice. It's his authentic expression and style. Most people aren't offended. Even those who are offended start to accept and rely on the fact "that's just who he is." As I've said, it would be jarring and completely inauthentic if Oprah walked on stage or began an interview with cursing and swearing. That Brand Voice is not consistent with her personality and would have everyone confused and shocked.

In short, your Verbal Identity guidelines should contain the following components:

- Brand Voice definitions
- Before and after examples of words that are aligned with the Brand Voice
- Tone and manner
- Grammar and syntax
- Writing style guidelines

BRAND ASSETS

Once you approve the final round of Visual Identity refinements, it's time to ask your brand designer to create all the artwork and files, known as your Brand Assets. Here is a useful checklist of the items to be included in your Brand Assets.

- Logo Suite
  - Artwork files (.ai, .eps format)
  - Viewable files (.jpg format)
  - Transparent (.png format)
  - Color
  - Black and White
- Typography/Fonts
  - Typography Style—Print
  - Typography Style—Web
- Color Palette
  - RGB (Red, Green, Blue) color codes
  - CMYK (Cyan, Magenta, Yellow, Black) color codes
  - Pantone color codes
  - Hex (web color codes)
- Patterns/Graphics
  - Artwork files (.ai, .eps)
  - Viewable files (.jpg)
  - Transparent (.png)
  - Color
  - Black and White

BRAND GUIDELINES

Upon completion of your Brand Identity, ask your branding partner to design and produce your Brand Guidelines. Brand Guidelines can be as simple as a one-page Visual Identity Guideline all the way to a thirty- or forty-page Brand Guidelines.

In addition to any Brand Strategy components that you'll want included in your Brand Guidelines, you might want to include other aspects, such as:

- Masterbrand Logo (minimum space, minimum size, and logo misuse)
- Sub-brand Logos
- Logo Placement (Sample Mock-ups)
- Color Palette (primary and secondary colors, color pairing, color gradients)
- Typography Style (Print and Web) and Typesetting Examples
- Photography Guidelines (categories, style, and recommended treatments or filters)
- Mock-ups of Brand Touchpoints, e.g., T-shirts, Mug, Stationery, Notebook, Social Media Cover, Trade Show Banner
- Graphic Elements or Patterns

PHASE THREE: BRAND MARKETING
WHERE ART AND SCIENCE PLAY TOGETHER

The third phase (after you complete your Brand Strategy and Brand Identity) is called Brand Marketing. Brand Marketing is simply that—marketing your brand to build an audience, generate leads, monetize your services and products, and position you as the go-to company in your industry. You may need a new website, marketing funnels, marketing collateral, product sheets, trade show materials, presentation slides, product packaging, or even new brand videos.

Every business has different marketing needs that will vary, depending on budget and optimal channels for getting in front of its target audiences. It will be overwhelming and cost-prohibitive to implement every single brand touchpoint through every single channel all at once. It's for this reason that I recommend prioritizing your Brand Marketing activities by implementing the brand touchpoints that will directly impact your revenue potential or business goals. For example, if your customers and prospects interact with your brand in a physical space (e.g., a retail shop or office), creating a branded retail experience will be more important than if your customers and prospects are exclusively online, in which case, you may not need printed business cards or marketing collateral, trade show banners, or building signage.

Here's a simple three-step process to prioritize your Brand Marketing activities and brand touchpoints.

Step One. List

Make a complete list of the various Brand Marketing activities and Brand Touchpoints and organize them along three phases of the customer life cycle:

- Pre-Purchase (touchpoints prior to a sale)
- Purchase (touchpoints at the time of sale)
- Post-Purchase (touchpoints after the sale)

Step Two. Prioritize

Rank each Brand Marketing activity and Brand Touchpoint on a scale of one to ten for Impact on Business (where one=Low Impact and ten=High Impact). Then rank each one on a scale of one to ten for Degree of Implementation (where one=Difficult and ten= Easy).

Impact on Business
(1=Low Impact, 10=High Impact)

Degree of Implementation
(1=Difficult, 10=Easy)

_____

_____

_____

_____

_____

As you can see from the next chart, when you populate each Brand Marketing activity and Brand Touchpoint on the chart, it will determine where to best focus your time, money, and energy. For example, if your Product Sheets are rated ten (High) on Impact on Business and ten (Easy) for Degree of Implementation, these are your "Quick Wins." However, if you want to create a mobile app for your business, but it will have a one rating (Low) for Impact on Business and a one rating (Difficult) for Degree of Implementation, then it's a Brand Touchpoint that you can clearly ignore and never prioritize.

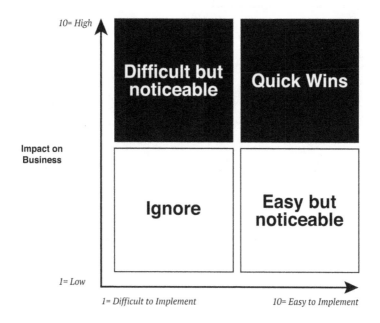

Step Three. Map

Add your prioritized Brand Marketing activities and Brand Touchpoints and map them along the customer experience journey: Pre-Purchase, Purchase, and Post-Purchase.

	Pre-Purchase	Purchase	Post-Purchase
Quick wins (High-Priority Brand Touchpoints to Implement within 30-45 days)	Brand Touchpoint Brand Touchpoint Brand Touchpoint	Brand Touchpoint Brand Touchpoint Brand Touchpoint	Brand Touchpoint Brand Touchpoint Brand Touchpoint
Difficult but noticeable (High-Priority Brand Touchpoints to Implement within 45-180 days)	Brand Touchpoint Brand Touchpoint Brand Touchpoint	Brand Touchpoint Brand Touchpoint Brand Touchpoint	Brand Touchpoint Brand Touchpoint Brand Touchpoint

At this point, I have good news and bad news for you.

First, the good news. If you've been following along in this book, you'll quickly realize that you have all the tools you need to create, build, and manage your brand in the marketplace. And, while the marketplace will change or your business will change, you have a solid foundation on which to build. You've adopted an empowering mindset for building a brand. You have the philosophy and "way of thinking" about building a brand, even if your brand needs to pivot, course-correct, or evolve over time.

Now, the bad news. You're just getting started. Building a brand is not a "one-and-done" activity. It's more common than not that a brand takes on a life of its own. You most likely won't be able to think about branding the same way ever again. More importantly, it's now time for you, your team, and your entire organization to start living your brand. Because this is where the rubber meets the road when it comes to Brand Authenticity.

CHAPTER ELEVEN

Living Your Brand

BE > DO > HAVE

In chapter three, I mentioned my exposure to personal development courses at Landmark Education. While there are several concepts that I learned and continue to apply that have shaped both my life and business, there's one fundamentally paramount concept that sets the tone for the topic of "Living Your Brand."

At one event I attended, the course leader invited us to consider that most people go through life following this sequence: they "do" certain actions in order to "have" certain things, so that they can ultimately "be" a certain way in life.

Do ➔ Have ➔ Be

As I sat in my chair at the course, I began to apply this construct to my life at the time. Sure enough, I was living life on this path, particularly since my twenties when I moved to New York City. Many New Yorkers have heard the phrase: "if you can make it here, you can make it anywhere." And, I was hungry to "make it." I engaged in certain actions ("the doing"), such as getting a degree from a reputable university, landing a good job, making money, and networking with the right people. I went to New York University and earned my degree in Organizational Behavior and Communications. I worked at several companies, hopping from job to job so that I could continually make more money. I met many new people and each additional connection led me to new opportunities. Eventually, I was in a career working with the top advertising agencies, design firms, and brand consultancies in Manhattan. Making "decent" money. The choreographed set of actions enabled me to obtain ("the having") certain things: my own apartment, a car, nice clothes, and whatever my desires were at the time. And truth be told, I also started to "have" more debt, more material stuff, and more headaches.

But, I was *not* happy. Rather, I felt empty and lost.

I recall one night when my best friend asked me why I was unhappy. On the outside, he thought I seemed so together. He said, "You're attractive, have your own home, and a career." He assumed that I was happy.

Landmark Education taught me that there's an empowering way to approach living life, and it starts with who you're "being."

The distinction "Be > Do > Have" challenges us to reverse the direction by starting with who you're "being," which will then direct (perhaps even pre-determine) the actions you take ("doing"), and the things you obtain ("having").

Be ➡ Do ➡ Have

It never occurred to me that I could "be" happy right now—even before having certain things and *without* doing certain things. This fundamental mindset shift altered the trajectory of my life. If it weren't for this distinction, I would probably still be waiting to one day be happy.

As it relates to your brand, instead of focusing on the "doing, having, and being" of branding, I invite you to build a brand by "being, doing, and then having." I apply this framework of thinking in my brand and in the advice I offer my clients with their brands. For example, you can do all the right things to build and have the perfect branding from logos, colors, images, and messaging. But, if you and your company aren't "being" your brand, then all the hard work, energy, and investment you've made to create your brand will be compromised.

Why? Because, if all the branding work isn't consistent with the experience your target audiences have with you in the marketplace, then they will perceive you and your company, either consciously or subconsciously, as inauthentic—and therefore, untrustworthy.

And, at the end of the day, we buy from brands that we know, like, and trust.

Creating a brand and earning people's trust takes work. Challenging circumstances are inevitable—whether it's a negative review, unexpected feedback, a disgruntled client or customer. Knowing this can and will happen, I want to prepare you with three guiding principles for living your brand, so that you can protect the coveted trust that you've earned from the people who have bought into your brand.

GUIDING PRINCIPLE ONE: OWN IT

I think the days are numbered for gurus and unquestioned thought leaders in the entrepreneurial world and businesses at-large. There are so many ways that companies can express themselves, and the landscape is overflowing with smaller companies and less-famous people to learn from. Let's not support an environment where people believe that there is only one guru to emulate, or one path to follow for success.

When you create a brand, it's your brand to live. So, find your own path and own it. It's okay to be inspired by companies that are ahead of yours or represent something you wish to embody in your brand. However, don't compromise or sacrifice the integrity of your own brand by trying to be something that you're not. Regardless of what the "experts" or "gurus" proselytize.

On occasion, I'll witness someone clearly modeling (or even copying) other seemingly successful entrepreneurs and business owners. They'll think, "That company grew by launching an information product, so I, too, should launch an information product." Or, "that person is crushing it with webinars, so I too can crush it with webinars."

It's exceedingly common for us, as humans, to want to compare ourselves to others. It's easy for us to convince ourselves that we need to do the same things as them if we want to achieve the same level of influence, financial success, or fulfillment. The truth is, when you truly live your own brand, your company's journey will look completely different from the journey of another company.

It's an incredible feeling to be inspired by companies that are achieving extraordinary results, but don't be afraid to embark upon your own path, innovate your own journey, or revolutionize or disrupt products or services that could better solve people's problems or improve their lives.

That said, finding your own journey is a process in and of

itself. No one, including myself, can simply tell a company who they should be as a brand, without understanding the data points that have defined and shaped them today, but also the insights and vision that gives a future glimpse of what your brand could be if it were fully expressed as an authentic brand.

Living your brand starts with you.

As you recall in chapter one, I define branding as the process of creating, shaping, and influencing a *desired* perception. However, there's the other side to this concept that is critically important in the context of living your brand and owning it.

You must first have that same perception of yourself.

Having an authentic brand sets the foundation for you to become your brand. Once you've set up clear brand guidelines, commit to following them. Really own the features and characteristics that make your brand distinctive. Now that you've identified the space that your brand occupies, establish a sense of pride in it and take ownership of it.

It's a big commitment to own your brand. I hope that you can see how branding can positively affect, and even transform, many areas of your business. The time, energy, and money you put into living your brand will come back to you multifold.

In short, "owning" your brand is really about "being" your brand, and never looking back.

GUIDING PRINCIPLE TWO: FOSTER IT

You can have the best branding in the world, but if you are not fostering it, the path to success will be compromised. Fostering your brand is a process in which you're regularly closing the gap between your desired perception, i.e., your brand, and the reality of who you are. In doing so, you walk closer to "being" your brand as opposed to just "having" a brand. It's in this alignment that real power emerges. That's when you'll experience the results you're seeking. That's when you're able to effortlessly move through all of the steps of gathering raving fans, engaging with your ideal clients and customers, and building a brand that is rewarding and fulfilling. This is truly the definition of being an authentic brand, because there's no "trying" to be a brand. You just are your brand.

In my experience, I've had a few private clients who were financially and intellectually ready to uplevel their brand. However, they were not successful at fully integrating and fostering their brand each and every day. I would argue that they weren't emotionally ready to not only own their brand but foster it. Inevitably, it's for this reason that they didn't achieve the massive success that was available to them. As an analogy, think of it this way. Imagine taking a friend to do a complete personal image and wardrobe makeover. After the process, they look completely transformed—a new hairstyle, new accessories, and new wardrobe. But in their mind, they still lack confidence. Their inner self doesn't align with their outer self. They look the part, but they're not *being* the part. It's not fully integrated into their being. As a result, they look uncomfortable and misaligned.

A useful tool to foster your brand is to make everyday decisions based on your brand. In other words, you would ask yourself, "Is this on-brand or off-brand for me?" When you practice making decisions based on your brand rather than how you feel on a given day, you'll quickly integrate your brand and easily filter out everything that is NOT your brand. You'll use your brand as a lodestar that guides your decision-making process, and therefore the actions you take, the people you interact with, and the activities you participate in.

Another useful and practical tool, especially for service-based brands is to use your Brand Values to determine if a client is a "fit" for your company. I learned very early on in my business that not everyone with a credit card is meant to be your client. In fact, taking on clients who are not a fit ends up depleting your soul and energy. I've personally turned down business because my Brand Values weren't aligned with a prospect. It didn't matter to me whether or not my team could easily fulfill on the project needs or if the prospect was willing to pay for my company's services. I'd rather turn down business because "revenue, for revenue's sake" is not in my values system. Rather, integrity, collaboration, and mutual respect are more essential to me than money.

In short, "fostering" your brand is about the actions (the "doing") you take (and don't take) that are consistent with your brand.

GUIDING PRINCIPLE THREE: MANAGE IT

You might have speculated that the third guiding principle is not about who you're "being" or about the actions you're "doing" to live your brand. Instead, it's about "managing" the brand that you "have"...as a result of who you're "being" and what you're "doing."

Think of your brand as a living, breathing entity. Let's face it. Every day, we evolve as human beings. As business owners, we constantly learn, grow, and develop. As brands, we interact with people—whether those people are clients, customers, channel partners, affiliates, employees, or potential employees. Much like an organism, your brand will naturally need to evolve over time. Your brand is not a destination, and "living your brand" is not a linear, static, or one-time activity.

I believe an instrumental part to successfully living your

brand is to stay deeply connected with and closely dialed into the response your target audiences have when they interact with your brand. Simply put, this means "listening" to them.

To be clear, I'm not referring to listening to the marketplace in order to have them dictate who you are as a brand. Rather, I'm suggesting listening to the marketplace to evaluate if your *desired* perception is actually the perception that's out there. It's about determining if you're successful at influencing and shaping your desired perception; or, if you need to make changes or course corrections along the way.

Brand Management comes in one or both of the following methods:

PASSIVE BRAND MANAGEMENT

A passive approach to managing your brand is simply being observational. This can look as informal or fluid as you want. For example, if you have a retail or in-person brand experience, observe how your prospects or customers interact with your brand. Observe their body language and facial expressions. Can you tell if they are excited or bored? Are they engaged or confused? Pay attention to the questions they ask or the concerns they have. Are they curious and intrigued? Or are they frustrated and annoyed? While this approach to brand management is qualitative, it can still be a powerful tool if you're able to document your observations and spot themes or trends in what you're observing.

ACTIVE BRAND MANAGEMENT

For a quasi-scientific and active approach to Brand Management, you can simply ask your target audiences what they think about your brand. You can either set up one-on-one time to talk with them and ask a series of open-ended questions, or you may decide to conduct a survey eliciting both open-ended and Likert-scale type questions.

But, here's a pro tip. Don't ask or survey your clients about how "satisfied" they are about your brand. That's a different type of research report under the umbrella of a Customer Satisfaction survey. While that study might be useful to determine how well your customers are satisfied, this information is not useful for you in the context of managing your brand. Instead, I recommend a simple survey design that generates actionable insights to help with managing your brand. It's called the "Importance versus Performance Grid."

Here's how it works.

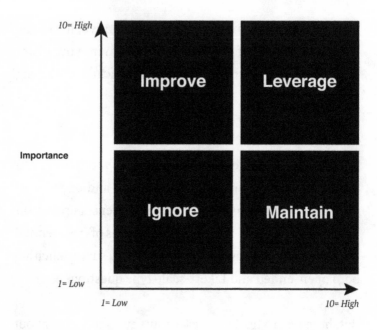

Step One

Brainstorm a list of all the features or benefits that are important to your target audiences. Then, shorten the list and narrow them down to eighteen to twenty of the strong features or benefits. For example:

Features or Benefits

Good value for the money

24-Hour Customer Service

Flexible Payment Plans

User-Friendly Website

Access to Chat Feature Online

Fair Return or Refund Policy

Step Two

Create a survey that asks your customers to rate the importance of each of these features or benefits AND how well they perceive your company is doing in these areas on a scale of one to ten (one=low and ten=high). Using our examples above, here's an example of a completed survey.

Features or Benefits	Importance (1=Low and 10=High)	Performance (1=Low and 10=High)
Good value for the money	8	2
24-Hour Customer Service	9	10
Flexible Payment Plans	1	2
User-Friendly Website	9	1
Access to Chat Feature Online	1	8
Fair Return or Refund Policy	4	5

Step Three

Populate the answers on the Importance versus Performance Grid to determine the aspects of your brand to manage. As you can see once the chart is populated, "24-Hour Customer Service" is an aspect of this company's brand that should be leveraged, because it's really important to its customers. On the other hand, a "User-Friendly Website" is really important to its customers, but the company is not performing that well in this area. This should be prioritized and improved right away. "Access to Chat Feature Online" is not important to this company's customers at all, but the company is clearly doing well in this area. This might be a nice feature to have, but it's not going to move the needle forward, so it's best to simply maintain this feature. Finally, any items in the bottom left quadrant are of low importance and considered low performance. You could improve these areas, but they won't make a difference in improving your brand, so ignore these items. It's a waste of time.

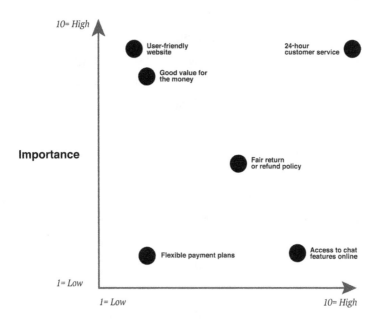

In short, "managing" your brand is about creating a feedback loop between your brand and your target audiences to ensure the perception that you "have" matched the desired perception that you want.

A WAY OF BEING

All the teachings in this book are ingredients for building a brand. Throughout this book, I've referred to branding as a discipline or a "process." But, truthfully, when it comes to "living your brand," I believe it's about relating to branding as a "way of being." Similar to Buddhism philosophy—"a

LIVING YOUR BRAND · 235

way of life"—I firmly believe that branding is very much the same. I encourage you to adopt living your brand as a choice in how you operate day-in and day-out in your business... and even in your life, in general.

Sure, you can use branding as a magic pill or a "get-rich-quick" tool with no regard for whether or not you're making an impact on people. You can use branding to manipulate people to buy from you once (or maybe a few times). You can pretend to live your brand on the outside but be something entirely different behind closed doors.

But why would you want to?

I truly believe that you will propel much further in business (and with less effort and discord) when you simply live your brand—everywhere and always.

Your brand can be the most powerful asset of your business. So own it, foster it, and manage your brand and it will pay out dividends multifold.

Conclusion

If you're going to spend the time, energy, and money to build an authentic brand, please heed this advice.

Your brand will NOT resonate with everyone.

Will you be okay with that?

If you're concerned that you'll make less money because you'll piss off some people by broadcasting your authentic self through a loudspeaker—remember, not everyone with a credit card is meant to be your client or customer. Inevitably, you will trigger some haters. People may spread negative messages about you through hate mail, social media, or other public forms of defamation. Don't focus on that low vibrational frequency of energy. That energy is about them, not you.

I believe you'll be better off not taking money from people

who are not your ideal target audiences. In contrast, you'll appreciate your business more when you're truly helping the people you are meant to serve.

Now, if you've gotten this far in the book and you're still telling yourself that you don't need a brand—let alone an "authentic brand"—this next part is especially dedicated to you.

Whether you're in the early stages of business and just starting to earn money, or you're a seasoned CEO business owner who's achieved massive success *without* branding, you might take comfort in knowing that I agree with you.

There's no question that you can build a business and make a lot of money through great marketing and sales. You might end up spending a little bit of extra time on trial and error. You may invest more in marketing or advertising. You may have to resort to gimmicky marketing tactics or succumb to high-pressure, manipulative sales tactics to acquire customers. But, I strongly argue that in the end, it's really not about the massive business or the ridiculous amount of money you're able to make.

It's about the opportunities that are *not* available to you, because your brand is inauthentic.

It's about being able to put your head on your pillow each

night, knowing that you're building a business that is integrous with you and what you stand for.

It's about being fulfilled in your business and knowing that your brand is making a lasting difference in people's lives.

So, stop chasing likes and followers. Stop measuring success by money and top-line revenue. Instead, measure your brand's success based on real results, real value, and real impact.

And, while you now have the tools rooted in art and science to create an authentic brand, you're only just getting started.

Don't just create a brand...it's time for you to live it!

Acknowledgments

To all the people near and dear to my heart (you know who you are) who believed in, empowered, and unconditionally loved me; and, in contrast, to those who bullied, teased, or underestimated me, I'm eternally grateful because all of you played a part in my journey towards authenticity and self-discovery to help me remember who I am.

About the Author

RE PEREZ is a seasoned Brand Strategist, author, keynote speaker, and CEO of Branding For The People, an award-winning branding firm for high-growth entrepreneurs and expanding small to midsize businesses. Utilizing his diverse expertise in Fortune 500-level branding, forward-thinking design, and marketing best practices, Re has built a respectable reputation and proven track for creating market-leading brands across 100+ different industries and professions. His clients often credit him for doubling, tripling, or quadrupling their business and impact.

Re's storied career includes senior-level positions at top global branding firms, including BrandLink, Interbrand, Reputation Management Institute, Siegel+Gale, and TMP Worldwide where he gained invaluable experience consulting to AREVA, Abbott Nutrition, Amersham Biosciences, GE Money, Lilly, Nalco, Novo Nordisk, Nielsen Company, TD Ameritrade, and Xerox.

As a Keynote Speaker, Re electrifies audiences everywhere by bringing forward-thinking insights, actionable content, and practical tips for creating authentic brands. His speaking portfolio consists of major entrepreneurial conferences including: Amazing's SellerCon, Baby Bathwater, EO's Global Leadership Conference, Digital Marketer's Traffic & Conversion Summit, Infusionsoft's ICON and PartnerCon, Ontraport's Ontrapalooza, and Social Media Week Austin, (to name a few). He is interviewed on podcasts and is a faculty teacher for the Growth Institute.

Re holds a degree in Organizational Behavior and Communications from New York University. He has lived in Florida, New York City, Dubai, and San Diego, but currently resides in Austin, Texas.